Allelon:
One Another

Understanding Body Life through the One Another Passages

R F Pennington

Copyright 2010 by the author of this book, R F Pennington.
The book author retains sole copyright
to his contributions to this book.
Published 2010.
Second Edition. Published 2013.
Printed in the United States of America by Lightning Source Inc.

Cover photo by Dee Pennington.

All Scripture quotations are from the New American Standard
Bible © 1975, Lockman Foundation. All Greek Dictionary
citings © 1981, Lockman Foundation. Reproduction permission
granted through Fow1dation Press Publications,
publisher for the Lockman Foundation.

This book published by BookCrafters,
Joe and Jan McDaniel.
SAN 859-6352
bookcrafters@comcast.net

ISBN 978-1-937862-24-4
Library of Congress Control Number 201291927

Copies of this book may be ordered at
www.bookcrafters.net
and other online bookstores.

Dedication

Lots of Help! Therefore, lots of praise. Nuther Words: Dedication!

First, and foremost, a thanks to my Dad, Boyce. One who taught speech for a half century, he was my first proof reader and my toughest critic. I can still remember him saying, "People are who and things are that!" when correcting my many grammatical errors, leaving my colloquialisms alone. I should have graciously replaced his red ink pen for him. He has recently received a transfer to the Home Office and is waiting for me. His inability to walk (and now, mine) the last few years before he left prompted us to suggest, on his last day here, that we would take a walk together when I next see him.

To my brothers and sisters in my home church who took the time to read, correct, encourage and fund this work. Proverbs 27:17 is played out once again: Iron sharpens iron, so one man sharpens another.

Tim and Natalie Magistro
Richard and Viva Kemp
Brian VanDerWege
Bill and Joyce Butt
Daniel Harrigan
Buddy Kemp

Table of Contents

Foreword..1
A(n all too) Common Church..5
Body Life...12
Ekklesia -A People, Not a Place..16
Ministry Giftedness: The Bible says, "Yes!"......................................25
The Body: Harmony & Peace..38
The Body: Encouraging, Teaching, Admonishing,
Confessing & Prayer..47
The Body: Forbearing, Forgiving, Comforting & Kindness...60
The Body: Being Servants, Submissive & Hospitable...............79
The Body: Not Passing Judgment, Lying, Speaking Evil,
Challenging or Envying...88
The Body: Welcoming & Loving..102
And If Your Brother Sins. 118
Final Thoughts on Body Life...145

Foreword

I see the title of the book and can read the author's name, but who in the world is he and what makes him qualified to write anything I might be interested in?

Good question. I ask the same thing before I reach for a book and spend what little time I have delving through it. To begin with, I'm a preacher--or maybe I'm not. Some would think not, for currently I occupy no official pulpit in any designated meeting house listed in the Yellow Pages of Anywhere, USA, yet I'm still doing the same things I did while I occupied those pulpits. While attending Sunset International Bible Institute and gaining a Bachelor's of Ministry from the Theological University of America, I preached for the Churches of Christ for just over a dozen years, first in a tiny Texas town, then on to the East Coast and off to the Left Coast.

My hat is off to the instructors at whose feet I sat. No doubt if you know them at all, you will undoubtedly 'hear' them in this work. They taught me that I Timothy 4: 16 is far, far more important than maintaining the status quo of beliefs and practices that so many churches have either clung to very tightly--or abandoned wholesale for something contemporary for contemporary's sake. Either of these satisfies nothing doctrinally. Doctrine comes from God's word, and must be wrestled with daily. Our lives must change.

This book precludes the idea of Sunday only Christianity. This stance also cost me my positions as pulpit minister. In no time since my leaving the official ministry have I ceased from leading and teaching individuals or small groups in homes, the way of God.

An item that has, by and large, disappeared from

Christianity is the idea of One Another in the Body Life of the local church. Many come in, sit down, go through the motion of devotion, deposit a check and leave. Many are not significantly changed by their Christian experience because they have not experienced Christianity. What you will find in these pages is what I believe the Scriptures teach on the idea of Body Life, which can only be arrived at if the right map is followed. That map is the Bible and the legend to that map is composed of the One Another commands found between Malachi and Maps. You should consult that road map while reading this book.

To further prepare, we must examine what is meant by body, and the gifts that God gives to those in His body. Then, we'll turn to how the members of the body through gifts and Biblical principles truly edify one another. Can this book be used to teach others in a setting such as a house group or a Bible class? Yes, one will find helpful seed questions at the end of most chapters.

Please bear with my wording. In using some terms (such as sanctuary for auditorium, or Pastor to mean Preacher or Minister), I will be using them in a way that some church folks or denominations just don't use. I don't mean to raise eyebrows or, at worst, alienate the reader. I do intend to reach out to all flavors of Disciples with one single plea: get back to what God intended when he had His Bible written.

Enough written. I do not invite you to share my beliefs simply because they are in print. I do invite you to read this, read the passages, and then between you, your church family, and God, decide how you will carry out that which has been mandated. We are members of One Another and, therefore, are mandated to pursue, not hinder, these One Another commands.

OK, well, a couple of more items. I've used standard abbreviations for Bible books, which shouldn't pose too great a threat. If a verse is cited and an *f* placed after the verse, it means the next verse: e.g. Jno 3:16*f* means John chapter 3, verses 16 and 17. Two *ff*s means keep going till the thought is played out--usually 3 or 4 more verses.

Bracketed numbers, e.g. [5], means there's an endnote

at chapter's end that will contain additional information. All Greek words appear in their English transliteration.

OK, Brothers and Sisters, everyone grab your hats! Sisters, don't forget your gloves and let's everyone go to church!

A(n all too) Common Church

Gustavo had a funny sounding name to most folks. He was a bit strange, though no one could definitely put a finger on it. Perhaps it was the way he dressed. Some thought it his color blindness and the fact that he lived alone with no one to help him coordinate his clothes. And that was another thing that kept folks wondering--why in the world would someone in their late thirties or early forties not be married? Had he ever been married? Divorced perhaps? Were there kids we didn't know anything about? As hard as they tried, folks just couldn't get the information they craved.

Perhaps it was the way he talked to you on Sunday mornings. He had only been a member of our church for a few months, but was already taking it upon himself to be some sort of greeter. There you'd be, trying to get into the doors of the church building, running about three minutes behind, and Gustavo would be halfway out the door, grabbing your hand and wanting to talk! Then, when he did engage you in conversation, he would cock his head to the side when he was listening and sort of bob his head. At times it was enough for whoever was talking to lose their train of thought.

Gustavo had some strange things to say in Bible discussion class. His religious vocabulary, at times, sounded like it came from another planet--sort of a Heinz 57 of all kinds of religious groups. He seemed to be stuck on the fact that angels did this and angels did that and folks in Bible discussion class almost hated for him to raise his hand and talk. One Sunday morning, one of the deacons in the back of the classroom hooked his thumbs together and made little angel wings with his fingers when Gustavo raised his hand. It cracked the back row up. Some figured that Gustavo saw the little angel flying about, but it didn't seem to stop him from saying what he wanted to get off his chest that morning. Sure as the world, angels figured into his comment.

Gustavo was baptized by old brother Whitley. One really wondered where Whitley would find these people. He still owned an auto salvage yard out on the west end of town, and he was always giving jobs to folks like Gustavo. Well, to be sure, they weren't exactly criminals with tattoos and ponytails, but they were sort of the underclass, work-by-the-day kind. Sure, folks handed it to old brother Whitley for his endeavors, but man, what a menagerie of folks he could bring to church!

Some wanted handouts upon their first visit to the church services. Ask them questions about what they were after or hoped to gain by attending our church and you could get an answer ranging from 'A better life' to 'A better job' or even comments about how this would look to their mother in law or parole officer! Some wouldn't make it back a second trip, especially the ones looking for a handout. Quite a number wouldn't come to Bible discussion class, saying it was too hard to understand what was being talked about. Most everyone was just sure that all of them could dress a little better for church. Imagine blue jeans and t-shirts for church! Anyway, Gustavo was one of Whitley's folks.

One must admire Gustavo for his gusto. He's always wanting to hang around the building in his spare time (which is all the time, according to the secretary), setting up chairs and fixing communion. Folks aren't altogether comfortable with Gustavo setting up the communion. He's made quite a few comments about using wine instead of grape juice. Guess everyone is just afraid that they'll show up and wine will be in the communion cups instead of grape juice. Come to think of it, Gustavo hasn't been hanging around the church building lately as much as he used to. In fact, there have been several Sundays that he has missed. Reminds everyone of a lady that used to come with her kids.

Been so long since she's been at church that no one can quite remember her name. Most think that it is Billie, though some remember it as Betty. Folks tried and tried to find out if she was married and coming by herself, divorced or never been married. All attempts to find out were met with finely tuned evasive answers. We couldn't scrouge answers from her kids.

No one can really remember who studied with this lady or initially reached out to her. Seems that she just showed up one morning for church, with her kids in tow, and responded to the invitational altar call. Just like that!

No one really knew who she was or what avenue she came out of. At best, she would only come on Sunday mornings. If she sat in your area you soon learned that if you were going to hear a thing the pastor said, you'd better secure another place before it all started! Anyway, when she filled out her response card, she only put her name, kids' names and their telephone number--no address. We all figured that she didn't want to be bothered with visits from the visitation committee. Everyone has their different space requirements.

One Sunday morning, she responded a second time to the invitation, maybe about six months after she started coming. Towed all those kids down front and talked to the preacher for what seemed like an eternity. Worship leader had to lead all six verses of *Just As I Am* and then go on to two more songs. We remember that Sunday well, for one of the two air conditioners was on the fritz. We sang till we were red faced, then, to top everything off, the pastor got up and led a prayer of generalities, hardly mentioning her name! Man, we would have given anything to know what that lady told him! Most remember that particular Sunday as about the last time anyone ever saw her. No one knows of anyone who tried to contact her along the way. Remember, we only had her phone number and not an address. Things like that would surely warrant a personal visit, not an impersonal phone call.

Seems a shame, really, when there are some other brethren that you would like to see disappear instead of Billie (or Betty?). Sure, her kids were rowdy, but Billie herself was sort of quiet and never got in anyone's business. Not so with the Cumberlands. They give well, and seem to be in the middle of everything the church is into, but at times it is their way or the highway. More folks have received a tongue lashing complete with Bible verses from those two--and sometimes both at the same time. Let's put it this way: if something comes up that is important, sudden, or even out of left field, the church heaves a big sigh of relief when the Cumberlands show no interest in it. If they do, the church holds her breath and wrings her hands! Want an example?

Two years ago, the couple passed away that gave the land to the church. Their house sat next to the building and was given also. We really didn't need the house, seeing that it would take more to repair the thing and fix it up than it was worth. Besides, the city said that after the land was deeded to us, it became nonresidential or some such legalese. To make a long story short, we had the house torn down, removed and turned the area into a lot for the kids to play in and for the church to have potlucks outside. Then we had the battle of the trees. Boy, do we remember that one!

Easy enough it seemed. Had a church meeting that included the question: did we, or did we not want a tree line on the east side as a sort of windbreak/privacy screen and boundary marker since we couldn't put up a fence, again according to the city. Some suggested evergreen shrubs. Others suggested elms. Cumberlands wanted some sort of little Chinese Ornamental Miniature Evergreen Trees that they kept referring to as Comets! Well, elm trees are wild. Evergreen shrubs could be had for $12 apiece at the local nursery. The Chinese ornamental Comet whatevers were $60 bucks! By the time that meeting was over, there were folks with their feelings hurt while others had their feathers ruffled, but the decision was made: Each family, as they saw fit, would buy and plant an evergreen shrub. As luck would have it, the local nursery dropped the price by 25% since it was a church. Within a short time, two evergreens shrubs showed up, planted nicely along the front edge. Wouldn't you know it, by the next Sunday both evergreen shrubs were pulled up and piled in the comer of the lot. In their place, along with many others, was an entire ensemble of Chinese Ornamental Miniature Evergreen Trees!

To be sure, the Smiths and the Bartons were outraged that their trees had been uprooted. Elders' phones were ringing off the hook. The church's answering machine was full. To add insult to injury, the Cumberlands asked the church to pick up half the tab for the trees, $420 in all! To rub salt in the wound, the elders wrote a check for $150 to the Cumberlands and when the Smiths asked for reimbursement for their recently uprooted shrub, the elders told them to try and replant it at their house. By the following Sunday after the Great Ornamental

Comet Caper, a small bronze plaque about the size of a song book showed up by one of the Chinese Ornamental Miniature Evergreen Trees. It read, Trees Donated by the Cumberland Family.

All in all, we have a pretty good church family here. It's not growing by leaps and bounds but we do have our conversions every year. Sure, folks die and folks move away and our youth group has become smaller every year, but that is the national statistic. We love our minister. Our building is paid for. We are doctrinally sound and support a missionary family. Our potlucks come once a month and our Vacation Bible School once a year. We have a large ad every Saturday in the local paper advertising our worship service. Our Yellow Page entry is large and colorful. We are doing all, and being all, that we can be....No way...not even hardly!

If John doesn't tell us anything else in his first letter, he tells us this: that our vertical relationship with God is directly proportional to, and dependent on our horizontal relationship with our church family. The New Testament writers put it this way in the koine, or common, Greek: allelon. In English, One Another. Learn the word, for we will concentrate on this one Greek word, allelon, for the remainder of this book. In reality, for the remainder of our Walk here on earth.

We're familiar with the vertical passages that are found in First John. For comparison and illustration, we can reexamine them here:

1:6 If we say that we have fellowship with Him and yet walk in the darkness, we lie...

1:8 If we say that we have no sin, we are deceiving ourselves, and the truth is not in us.

1:10 If we say that we have not sinned, we make Him a liar, and His word is not in us.

What John is telling us is that we can say what we want to say, but in the end, God is both the rule maker and the ruler. That point qualifies Him, and Him alone, to decide who is in a relationship with Him and who isn't.

But we know that. For most, we have grown up with the idea of Thou shalt and Thou shalt not. We are constantly tuned into the vertical. That constant vigil on the vertical, perhaps, is the very reason that Body Life tends to take a second place in the church. Not intentionally, mind you. We don't set out to disregard one another. We simply become creatures of habit and tradition. But now, consider the following verses from First John:

2:9 The one who says he is in the light and yet hates his brother is in the darkness until now.

But we don't hate one another, do we? Of course not--or do we?

3:15 Every one who hates his brother is a murderer, and you know that no murderer has eternal life abiding in him.

Certainly we aren't murderers, are we? Of course not-- but are we? John has been talking in extremes. It was a first century Jewish thing: both ends of the spectrum, illustrated by exaggerations. Jesus did this when he talked about hating father and mother and camels going through eyes of needles and Pharisees straining gnats and swallowing camels. However, John does have a point to make concerning our interaction with one another here in this life--and the importance it brings to bear on our very relationship with the Father. If John 3:16 describes how God loved us, then First John 3:16 surely describes how we ought to love us:

We know love by this, that He laid down His life for us; and we ought to lay down our lives for the brethren. But whoever has the world's goods, and beholds his brother in need and closes his heart against him, how does the love of God abide in him? Little children, let us not love with word or with tongue, but in deed and truth. I Jno 3:16ff

John knows that, in reality, we will not get the chance to lay down our life for someone else. We talk about it in Sunday school. We explore the great 'what if' in small groups as we perpetually describe ourselves pushing another disciple out of the way of the proverbial bus--to our self-sacrificing demise. We go back to Jesus' sacrifice for us on Calvary..., but when we've done that, we've gone back to John 3:16, and left the command of First John 3:16: we ought. John doesn't leave us with the great What If. That's why verse 17 begins with the word but. But brings us back to everyday living: If you have, and your brother doesn't, then you are under obligation from God to participate in Body Life.

Body Life? Where did that come from? From John, just couched in other terms. From Paul, just couched in a body parts metaphor (I Cor 12). From James, as he talks about tongues and wars (Jas ch's 3&4). From Peter, as he talks about respecting the different groups of disciples (I Pet ch's 2&3). From Jude as he talks about snatching folks from a most dangerous fire. From Luke as he talks about the dangers of an evil and unbelieving heart (Heb 3).

From Jesus (Matt 19), as he gathers a group of young kids about him and uses them as an example of what we should be and how we should act...

Body Life

It's what was missing from our first three examples. As you read the three made-up-but-true accounts from an average church in an average town that meets on the corner of Faith & Grace, you may have had other names for the situations: oblivious to the obvious for the first two and way too intolerant for the last couple. For sure this is true, but they can all be bannered under the fact that an understanding of Body Life as one of the primary missions of the church, had long since been forgotten by those folks. Actually, it may be THE primary mission of the church.

Why the church? Why not some other way? Why not save us, and then let us go on our walk the best that we know how? Why the added responsibility of a family? Why are we our brother's keeper? Because there is a race that needs running--and finishing. Without the cohesiveness of the church, there would be no one left standing upon Jesus' return. I'm sure there are folks that think that they can do it on their own. I've also had my three children at one point or another in their growing up years envision that they could run away and make it just fine as a carnival barker. But however you see it, we have been left with, and mandated to participate in, the church. We are to be a part of it and partake of it. With that comes responsibility.

Responsibility presupposes preparation and qualification, and so it is in the church. We parents hold our 12 year olds more responsible than we do our toddlers. You might get upset with--but cannot hold responsible--a toddler for painting the davenport with watercolors, but you can a 12 year old. Why? Older? In a sense, yes. However, to peek behind the older reason is a dozen years of preparing that child to know that destruction of furniture and misuse of watercolors is a familial crime. That 12 year old was qualified to use water colors unsupervised.

Take the business world. Some of us make six figure incomes--and some of us do not! Within any given company there will be a scale of salaries. Folks will be entry level bottom and others will be maxed out in pay. Those who make the most will by and large have more responsibility. They hold that responsibility because they have a high level of training. Unless they have risen to the top through nepotism, or maxed out on the Peter Principle (or even through the Dilbert Principle), they will be the most qualified, also.

Now suppose you are a hot shot reporter for a business weekly magazine. Rising quickly in the business world is Widget Corp. They blew in to the business scene and really made a splash. Your assignment is to go spend the day with them, examine their place of business and interview as many types of workers as you can. The interview process goes something like this:

"As you can see, Mr. Reporter, we have a full daycare center complete with nannies and all the amenities of home, including a full set of water colors. Are you impressed so far? Every office is equipped with a personal vibrating foot massager for sore feet, too! Follow me to the water cooler, and if you have any questions, please feel free to ask. Oh, and look at the full fitness room and ..."

"I did have one question," as you interrupt the tour. "We keep passing this particular office and I was wondering just who occupies it and what role does he play in the corporation? You have given me a rundown on everyone else who occupies an office."

"Glad you asked that question. That office belongs to Mr. Speelik."

"Thank you. I can read the oversized, highly polished brass nameplate on the door. I guess I was hoping to get a little more in-depth information on the overall roll he might play around here. He sure does look important if oversized, highly polished brass nameplates are any indication of things."

"Mr. Speelik is our most qualified member in the whole corporation. Now if you will just follow me around the corner, we'll have a quick look at the informatics center..."

"Interesting. Qualified for what? What department or division does he head?"

"He doesn't head anything. He's simply just qualified. We send him to every seminar, he holds every degree and is licensed in every thing one can hold a license in. He is, as you might say, highly qualified. Actually, he doesn't do anything, for you see, he has no responsibility!"

By now, if you didn't say it you would think it: How absurd! Qualified to do nothing?!? No, we don't do that in the business world and the church shouldn't operate on that principle or practice either. If one is qualified, he or she is responsible. At least for now in our time together, entertain the thought that it is God who qualifies each and every individual in the church family.

Let's now dive as deep as we can to discover a line of reasoning to which the Bible is calling each and every disciple. This journey will first examine the church, what Jesus meant it to be and what we've often times made it to be. The second stop on the journey will involve the idea of Ministry Giftedness. The Bible clearly says, "Yes" to these non-miraculous gifts for Christians of all times and ages. Every disciple is God gifted, for God works through His people. Since it is a gift, we cannot take credit for what God has given us.

When we have examined the basis of Ministry Giftedness, we will see that we are not gifted for the sake of being gifted. There are assignments that accompany each gift. With those assignments come the responsibility from Heaven. Finally, under gifts we will explore the fact that all gifts belong to the body, the church. We are not islands unto ourselves and, therefore, we have an obligation one to another in the matter of giftedness. We will also see that our gifts are not for self-glorification.

The remainder of the study will travel through the various one another commands of the New Testament, allowing us to see what is to be the result of our ministry gifts. As with most studies of this scope and magnitude, it is suggested that the reader keep a Bible and a note pad close by. If a passage of Scripture is cited, take the time to read that passage at least once. This is intended, first and foremost, to be a Bible study.

Don't run at this point! Some folks will run at the mere

mention of Bible study. It is not the Bible that runs them off, but the word study. Forgive me for using that word. Call it Bible reading if it keeps you in your seat. I'll be honest, there have been times that the Bible has become dry and distant to me. There have been other times that it has come alive. I believe God, somehow, had His hand in the latter of making His word come alive. Take for instance, being stuck in Moab, Utah for three or four weeks with nothing to do except sit in the hotel room and wait for the phone to ring.

Mind you, this is pre-cell phone days--and pre Moab-is-a-hot-vacation-spot days. Nothing, NOTHING to do except read on this Gideon Bible in the room. Nuff said, for something opened up and the Bible once again came alive! Let it come alive again for you as you start this, um, study.

Ekklesia--A People, Not a Place

As a people for God's own possession, the church, we are called *out of, to* and *for*. *Out of* sin and Satan's grasp, *to* Heaven and its glory and *for* good works!

Sounds absurd to even slow down long enough to discuss this next concept. We've said over and over in our Bible classes and small groups that the church is the people and not the place. Our ministers, preachers, pastors and priests have (it is very much hoped) reiterated this time and time again from the pulpits on any given Sunday. Our outreach tracts and 'Welcome to the Family' brochures arranged neatly in our greeting area hardly get to page two before this concept is worded. However, our speech betrays us at highly emotional times, when we don't have a chance to think through the right words. Consider these real life scenarios:

A certain baptistry had been with a church family for almost seventy years. The original church building had been destroyed during the 1940's by a tornado that ripped through the outskirts of town one afternoon. The massive concrete baptistry had been the only thing left of the original building and was promptly moved closer to town and a whole new church meeting house had been built around it.

Time marched on and the baptistry cracked. Add to this the fact that the plumbing, now buried underground, was corroded and leaking. It had to remain empty, and only filled when the need arose. A meeting was called and it was suggested to jack hammer the concrete out, cut a hole in the outer wall, and remove the rubble. A state of the art fiberglass baptistry would replace it.

"What? Cut a hole in God's house? What? Remove what? Hey, this is my church, and I grew up in this church, and if you people want to tear into the church . . ."

Of course, the discourse went on and on. To be sure, it speaks of change and our keen ability to resist it, but it speaks also of our internal concept of church.

Another church built a building on the northeast side of town by the interstate many years ago. It was truly believed that the city would go that direction and the church building would then be in the midst of the populace. Thirty years later, the church found herself still meeting on the outskirts of town, for the town had grown directly away from the meeting house. It was proposed to move to town where the people were.

"But we love our church! You leaders wouldn't really sell our church, would you? I don't think that God ever dreamed of, or would approve of, the sale of his church."

The list could go on indefinitely (and sadly does), but enough has been written to see how our speech can betray us for, you see, it's hard to keep the church separate from the building for many reasons. However, the biggest reason of them all may be inadvertently from Preachers concerning Programs.

We've done the church, perhaps, a big disservice in this area. As ministers, we are tied to the pulpit--and moreover, the building. We've all preached those sermons about the church being the body of Christ, but often followed that with an appeal to "come to the workday next Saturday and spruce up the church." Often, our assessment of church involvement will revolve around how often we see someone at the building and how often they participate in the various programs held in that building. We habitually count the number of folks in church on any given Sunday. We're creatures of habit, but unless we work constantly and consistently on breaking that particular habit, it will continue to have far reaching implications in the church today. The world will not help us on that one. This definition came from Webster's New World Dictionary:

Church (fr Gk Kyriake oikia = Lord's House). 1. A building for public worship, especially Christian worship; 2. A religious service, usually Christian.

I won't hammer out something that has been presented a myriad of times. However, a review for some may have merit here. The word that we translate church in the New Testament is not Kyriake Oikia (a combination which is found nowhere in the New Testament so don't ask me where Noah Webster got it from!), but is nothing more than the common Greek compound word ekklesia - which was strangely missing from our Webster's definition. The two words that make up ekklesia are ek = out of, and klesis = called. It was used for all kinds of 'callings out of' in its day, and even presented in Scripture. Note the following words in bold type from Acts chapter 19 that are the Greek word ekklesia:

V 32 *"So then, some were shouting one thing and some another, for the **assembly** was in confusion, and the majority did not know for what cause they had come together."*

V 39 *"But if you want anything beyond this, it shall be settled in the lawful **assembly**."*

V 41 *"And after saying this he dismissed the **assembly**."*

Well, at least the translators did us all a favor by not sticking the English word church in there! But it does show how the word was used in the original language. Here, and in contemporary writings of the time, the word meant more than a gang of folks. They were called out- but always for a reason. A point of stress here--they were always called out for a reason. In verses 32 and 41, they were called out to take care of Paul and his traveling companions and put a stop to Jesus before He shut down their statue making. In verse 39, that would have been a legal assembly, called out to settle matters through the courts. In verse 41, their reason for being was put to bed.

Since Christians are called out (and we are), we must be called out for a reason (and we are). To drive point home, I've substituted the noun church in the following verses and made it a verb for the sake of illustration:

- God churched us in holiness (I Thess 4:7)
- We're churched through the Gospel (II Thess 2:14)
- We're churched into God's Kingdom & Glory (I Thess 2:12)
- We're churched to walk with God (Eph 4:1)

- We're churched with a holy calling based on Grace, not works (II Tim 1:9)
- God churched us (II Pet 1:10)

Just as the ancient Ephesians would have looked rather silly had they all been called out into the amphitheater, only to stand around scratching their first century heads (some did!), the lawful assembly would have looked even more silly all called into court--and nobody could figure out why! Whoever hired Mr. Speelik in our qualification illustration is a knucklehead. We in the church today are no different as far as our calling. We are called out--and for a reason. First, let's begin by an examination of what we are called out of.

Simply put, the world. But we know all too well that we wake up every morning and we're still on he same rock going around the same sun. We put on the same shoes and grab the same coffee mug, get into the same pickup and head to the same place and go about the same rat killing that we did the day before and the day before that and when we get up our feet still hurt and... One gets the picture. However, it isn't this spinning ball of carbon and silica that we are called out of. It is a kingdom exchange.

Kingdom carries with it the idea of king. King carries with it the idea of calling the shots. Whether we wish to admit it or not, every single person on the face of this earth is in a kingdom. The choice is two. And I do use the word choice. We're born into God's kingdom. Not the new birth through water and spirit that Jesus spoke of to Nicodemus, but birthday suit stuff. Somewhere along the way, we chose to leave God's kingdom and go elsewhere. It may not be as dramatic as the Prodigal Son that Luke records, but a kingdom exchange nonetheless.

Then we hear it. It's the calling of the gospel [1]. It may be called to us from godly parents or grandparents. It may be called to us through a coworker that cared enough to share Jesus with us--and keep sharing. It may be called to us through the rubble of a ruined financial life or a ruined marriage. It may be like a friend of mine's great uncle, who drove his wife 'to church' every Sunday for years.

Names escape me, so I'll call him Uncle Ben. Every Sunday, without fail, he drove Aunt Mabel to the church house. Every Sunday Uncle Ben would sit in the parking lot with his cigar and Sunday paper. Every Sunday Aunt Mabel would make sure the windows were open to the parking lot. Every Sunday the preacher would holler extra loud. Soon Uncle Ben was reading his paper less and listening to the sermon more. The same ol' songs that they sang over and over seemed to grow on him. He began to hum along. Once, Aunt Mabel heard him humming *Just As I Am* in the garage while working on the car. One Sunday morning during the sermon, after the distinct sound of a Buick door being shut in the parking lot, the church house doors opened ...

Move ahead forty years. One winter, Dee and I held Saturday night Bible studies in our home. It was only supposed to be for an hour and a half. At 11 p.m., we were still trying to flush folks out of our living room which had become crowded. I had a sermon to preach the next morning. I had a Bible class to teach the next morning. One particular Saturday night Granny showed up. Her granddaughter and new husband were part of our study. Granny just sat in the chair. My wife sat next to Granny and tried to share her Bible with Granny. Granny just sat, rocked, and stared ahead. This went on for weeks with Dee diligently at Granny's side, holding a Bible. After one particular study, when we were fielding comments and sharing, Granny spoke up for the first time. Everyone was listening. After all, she was a nonbeliever.

"I'm not much of a church goer and never have been. Pretty much thought it was a waste of time and energy. But, when I see the joy my granddaughter and her husband have over this thing, I had to come check it out."

Within weeks, Granny was baptized, putting on her Lord. Matthew records the eleventh hour worker. Granny went to the field at six minutes until midnight. Within a few short months her mind went. Within a year we stood in the church house around Granny's casket as she stood before God Almighty.

We're called out of the most hideous and vile kingdom ever known to man. For sure, Satan won't reveal the ugliness to most while still alive. That would be bad PR. Some recognize both the vileness of Satan and the call of the gospel--and heed the call. Let's now update our definition of the English word church:

Ekklesia - a people, not a place 1. Definition of the word as a noun: a compound word formed by ek "out of" and klesis "a calling." This was a common word of the first century to denote any calling out of a body of people, usually to attend to affairs of city or state (as in Act 19). This is the word that Jesus used to denote those He called out of the world for salvation.

Note the prayer that the apostle Paul had for the saints at Colossae:

*For this reason also, since the day we heard of it, we have not ceased to pray for you and to ask that you may be filled with the knowledge of His will in all spiritual wisdom and understanding, so that you may walk in a manner worthy of the Lord, to please Him in all respects, bearing fruit in every good work and increasing in the knowledge of God; strengthened with all power, according to His glorious might, for the attaining of all steadfastness and patience; joyously giving thanks to the Father, who has **qualified** us to share in the inheritance of the saints in light. For He delivered us from the domain of darkness, and transferred us to the kingdom of His beloved Son, in whom we have redemption, the forgiveness of sins.* Cols 1

He *what*-ified us? What was that bold word in the prayer? **Qualified!** There are some who were hoping that I would have forgotten to come back to this concept. Just as the Ephesian townsfolk were called out to the arena for a reason, we too are called from the kingdom of darkness for a reason. As we build the concept of Body Life, let's take the time to explore this reason. Nowhere is it stated more plainly and precisely for us than in First Peter chapter 2:

But you are a chosen race, a royal priesthood, a holy nation, a people for God's own possession, that you may proclaim the excellencies of Him who has called you out of darkness into His marvelous light; for you once were not a people, but now you are the people of God; you had not received mercy, but now you have received mercy.

That's it. Plain as punch. We're not called out to stand around. We're not called out to be entertained. We're not called out to dress up on Sunday morning. We're not called out to audit Christianity. We're not called out to eat. We're not called out to hear snappy sermons and spiffy choirs. We're not called to be the proxy church. We are called to proclaim.

Evangelism? No doubt, but before everyone packs up and heads to the uttermost parts of the earth (or simply just packs up and runs away!), consider the steps at home. We must first be functioning and vibrant here where we are. We must first be the body of Christ as Christ planned for us to be. We must hang the right sign out in the front of our church building. And what might that sign be?

Before you hit this paragraph, you had a sign in mind. We all do. We've fought long and hard battles over the correct name of the church. And why not, for signs do just that--they *signify*. We've split bodies over the sign out front. Anyone who can pick up a yellow pages can see that this is an ongoing battle with no end in sight. Jesus only authorized one sign. John recorded it for us in John chapter 13:

A new commandment I give to you, that you love one another, even as I have loved you, that you also love one another. By this all men will know that you are My disciples, if you have love for one another.

"That's a cheap shot!" one might say. No, it's Bible. Don't get me wrong, I'm all for identification through signs. Helps me when I'm traveling and doing a mailout. But I'm even more for taking a Bible approach to the body of Christ above identifying a building made of brick, stone, wood or mud. Look at the verse again. Isn't it neat that our Lord left us everything we need in order to be recognized as the church? To be sure, there is quite a bit wrapped up in that ever so conditional phrase, "if you have love for one another."

We need the right stuff in our worship on Sundays when the church comes together in a church building. We need the right attitude towards that worship. We need to say the right stuff and withhold the wrong stuff (which has its foundation in attitudes). We need to pay attention to what we are singing, not just singing 'cuz we (or the choir) sound good and the song has a spiffy tune. But when all is stripped away, the person outside looking inside needs to see the sign that Jesus authorized. No John chapter 13 sign, no recognition from outsiders. It can't be put any plainer.

As a minister, I have found nothing to be more true on a base level than the saying, "The seeker doesn't care what you teach or believe until he knows that you care." They simply don't--no matter how one carves it. We can jingle, cajole, trick or otherwise suck people into our edifices, but they won't stick for very long if we, by and large, don't care. When they find that we care: about them, their dreams, their fears, their hopes, their families, their direction in life; they will stick to us--and ultimately stick to the Lord--like glue.

And by the way, Jesus wasn't limiting his statement of love to the Sunday morning assembly in a church building on the corner of Faith & Grace. In fact, during his ministry on earth, Jesus never spoke of the assembling of saints on Sunday at all. Check it out and prove me wrong. He spoke of the church, but not the Sunday morning assembly. He had in mind Sunday morning at ten, but also Tuesday evening at seven and Friday noon. He had in mind the 24/7 church. He had in mind something that would be laid out in detail later by his apostles. He began a teaching, and expected others, guided by the Holy Spirit, to complete later. Consider the following passages:

"I have many more things to say to you, but you cannot bear them now. But when He, the Spirit of truth, comes, He will guide you into all the truth; for He will not speak on His own initiative, but whatever He hears, He will speak; and He will disclose to you what is to come. He shall glorifiy Me; for He shall take of Mine, and shall disclose it to you." Jno 16:12ff

"The first account I composed, Theophilus, about all that Jesus began to do and teach, until the day when He was taken up, after He had by the Holy Spirit given orders to the apostles whom He had chosen." Acts 1:1f

It's not that Jesus ran out of time. It's not that Jesus was operating on Plan B or some other contingency. It was his plan all along to start something and let the apostles finish carrying it out through the avenue of divine inspiration. Same holds true to his 'sign' command in John chapter 13 about loving one another. He set the command in motion and the inspired writers finished explaining everything we need in order to function under the identifying banner of love--our first step in homeland evangelism: Body Life and the One Another commands.

But remember, God never asked us to do anything that He didn't first qualify us to do. Please keep that thought in mind throughout the rest of the, um, study. He has asked us to carry out Body Life and qualified us through Ministry Giftedness. That's a comforting thought, isn't it: we are qualified by the one who asked us to do. We don't have to go off somewhere, scrounge or guess. The Master arranged it all--but with this heavenly arrangement, there is expectation.

Questions for thought or discussion:

1. Do you have a family concept of the church? If you don't, what hinders you from holding this concept?

2. Is it possible to fulfill all of your Christian works on Sundays? Some? What part or percentage?

3. In light of the purpose of the assembly, do you see yourself as more of a spectator or a participant?

4. Which is more important, attending the assembly or working together to build up one another relationships? What Scriptures did you base your answer on?

Endnotes:

[1] Jno 6:41-45. Also note in this passage the correlation between the Father drawing folks to Him in verse 44 and the teaching/calling/heard the Gospel in verse 45. Interesting...

Ministry Giftedness The Bible Says, "YES"

Speaking in tongues; healing the sick; raising the dead; casting out dem... Wait a minute! I'm not talking about miraculous gifts through the empowerment of the Holy Spirit. I'm talking about Ministry Giftedness! Miraculous gifts are a whole 'nuther subject, and that subject is all about confirming the Word. It's already confirmed and we can all go to bed on that one. I'm talking about empowering Christians for Christianity. We go to Romans for our two illustrations.

The first illustration is an inference, or the art of gathering information in the context and making a decision. We do it all the time, but it is outside the scope of this book to delve into all of the hermeneutical principles in play (the herme-what-ical?). One thing is for sure with an inference: if you get it wrong, something concrete in the context will contradict it. If you get it right, something in the context will affirm it! The first illustration comes from the first half of Romans chapter 1. You may want to take the time to read it.

Take the time to read it.

Did you read it?

Paul had not been to Rome yet when he wrote the Roman letter. To be sure, someone had been in Rome preaching the gospel of God, but not Paul. He had certainly tried to go.

Made plans to go many times, but as of yet it was a no go. He wanted to visit Rome for three reasons. The first was to preach to them. Not that they needed a lesson on salvation--for they already had obeyed the gospel. He simply wanted to hold what we would call today a gospel meeting or revival. The second reason he wanted to visit Rome was to 'obtain some fruit' from among the Roman Christians. Perhaps he wanted to pick up a traveling partner. Perhaps he wanted to expand the church through immersions. Whatever the specifics, Paul referred to it as fruit.

Thirdly, Paul wanted to impart spiritual gifts to the Romans so that they would be established. What kind of gifts? Spiritual gifts from the empowerment by the Holy Spirit. For what reason? Establishing, or grounding, the church in the middle of Pagan Central. What is the reason for miraculous gifts again? Confirm the word.

Now we infer from this wish of Paul's that to-date they had no miraculous gifts. Were they saved? Of course they were, chapter six tells us that. Were they the church of God? If they were saved they were! Besides, Paul calls them saints in Romans 1:7. They simply had no miraculous gifts and Paul wanted them to have miraculous gifts--those gifts that went outside the boundaries of time and space to effect something that no one can do of themselves, being bound by time and space. Romans 1:11 clearly spells out Paul's wish. Did they have any gifts? Yes. Chapter 12:

For through the grace given to me I say to every man among you not to think more highly of himself than he ought to think; but to think so as to have sound judgment, as God has allotted to each a measure of faith. For just as we have many members in one body and all the members do not have the same function, so we, who are many, are one body in Christ, and individually members one of another. And since we have gifts that differ according to the grace given to us, let each exercise them accordingly: if prophecy, according to the proportion of his faith; if service, in his serving; or he who teaches, in his teaching; or he who exhorts, in his exhortation; he who gives, with liberality; he who leads, with diligence; he who shows mercy; with cheerfulness.
Rom 12:3ff

Paul clearly called these gifts, but not the kind that break the bounds of time and space. Hang with me and let's clomp through this together. No withered limb would grow strong and straight with these types of gifts. No dead were to come out of the tombs with these types of gifts. No man born blind would suddenly and completely see with these types of gifts. No water was to become wine with these types of gifts, but they are gifts nonetheless.

And the gifts were there for a reason. They weren't there to 'wow' each other. Paul made that clear in verse 3. They weren't there to become dormant. Paul made that clear in verse 5. They were there in the Roman saints because they were members one of another and all made up one body in Christ. We call this the church. True in Rome and true where you are.

When the Bible speaks for our time and condition, we are committed to obey. If ministry giftedness is Bible indicated, it is Bible mandated. Its discovery, development and employment is not optional, nor is the hiding of these gifts not without consequences. Consider:

- Every disciple is God gifted.
- Every gift is accompanied by an assignment.
- Every gift is a body gift.
- Every gift is open to ministry development.
- Every gift is a sacred stewardship.

The fact of giftedness should not blow the disciple of Christ away. We have been running over and through ministry giftedness in our Sunday schools and sermons for decades. Look at the following phrases and Scripture notations and note how familiar they are to us:

- Eph 4:6 God works through His people
- Rom 12:3 God deals to each man
- I Cor 12:18 members set in the body as God pleases
- Eph 3:21*f* His power works in us
- Phil 2:13 God works in us
- Eph 4:7 to each one of us grace was given accordingly
- Eph 4:16 every joint supplies
- I Pet 4:10 as each has received

Jesus touched on giftedness from God. He didn't call giftedness *native ability* or *natural talent*, but tied it to native ability. It is found in the parable of the talents of Matthew chapter 25. Note the emphasized text:

*"And to one he gave five talents, to another, two, and to another, one, **each according to his own ability**; and he went on his journey."*

Just as an alternator in a truck is *part* of the electrical system, it is not *the* electrical system. Bunches of people are part of a dinner party, but you have to have food and little weenies on toothpicks to call it a party. Native ability is part of ministry giftedness, but is not the whole enchilada. God, who gave you the native ability in the first place, will add His final ingredient. The outcome is, you will be qualified. But we must always keep in mind (just as the early Christians had to with miraculous gifts) the three rhetorical questions that Paul asked the Corinthian church (I Cor 4:7):

- For who regards you as superior?
- And what do you have that you did not receive?
- But if you did receive it, why do you boast as if you had not received it?

Just as the three servants in Jesus' parable of the talents were qualified to do business, so are we qualified to do ministry within the body of Christ for the body of Christ. Just as the three servants had a responsibility and an accounting for their gifts, so we have the same. Just as the one was called in on the carpet for sidelining his gift, we will be also if we choose to sideline ours. That is the whole point of the lesson that Jesus was trying to give. We have known this. We have known it all along. We may not have thought out all the implications of this.

Jesus' whole point of the parable was to show us responsibility and accountability. Take the time to read Mark 13:34 and Luke 19:13 for further examples through parables. He didn't go into any detail or mention at all about the comparison of the three servant's financial business (or lack of) and what that translates to us today. Again, a quick look at the first two verses of Acts will remind us that Jesus didn't give us all teachings on all subjects while here on earth. Some were left, by God's design, to the apostles.

The statement was made that each ministry gift was a body gift. Nowhere is this illustrated better than in Ephesians chapter 4:

"But to each one of us grace was given according to the measure of Christ's gift... And He gave some as apostles, and some as prophets, and some as evangelists, and some as pastors and teachers, for the equipping of the saints for the work of service, to the building up of the body of Christ; until we all attain to the unity of the faith, and of the knowledge of the Son of God, to a mature man, to the measure of the stature which belongs to the fulness of Christ. As a result, we are no longer to be children, tossed here and there by waves, and carried about by every wind of doctrine, by the trickery of men, by craftiness in deceitful scheming; but speaking the truth in love, we are to grow up in all aspects into Him, who is the head, even Christ, from whom the whole body, being fitted and held together by that which every joint supplies, according to the proper working of each individual part, causes the growth of the body for the building up of itself in love."

Let's look back at Romans chapter 12. Let's make sure those weren't miraculous gifts. Look at the list carefully: Leading? - no, not miraculous. Showing mercy? - no, non-miraculous. Giving? - (don't understand everything I know about this fully, but) no, non miraculous. Teaching? - ditto, non-miraculous. Serving? definitely non-miraculous. Prophecy?-oops?!?

Just as our definition of 'church' has been hammered and altered over the centuries, so has our view of prophecy. Somewhere in popular church culture we gained the idea that to prophesy meant that the speaker had to predict the future. Just as all dimes are coins, not all coins are dimes. The strict definition of prophesy is forthtelling, not necessarily foretelling. It simply means to speak forth the will and word of God. Look back at some of your prophets in the Old Testament. Not everything they had to say was a prediction of the future. Plenty of times they burst upon their particular Old Testament scene and said, "You see what is going on around you? Here's the reason why..." They weren't looking forward, but backward!

Paul was simply speaking about those who speak forth the word of God. Who are they today? Preachers and teachers. But someone may ask, "Isn't that going a bit too far? I know that some have the native ability to preach, but are you saying that God has his hand in it somehow to add that something extra to a teacher or preacher to make it a gift?" Let me ask,

Allelon: One Another

"Why do we pray for reddy rekkalexions if we don't believe it?" We believe it. We've believed it all along [2].

Giving is another one. Non-miraculous, but how is it a gift? What part does innate ability and God have to play in giving? For sure it isn't miraculous. Miraculous giving would be if someone had $1 in their pocket, they pulled it out and gave it away and *viola* there was suddenly another dollar in their pocket! Let's be honest here. If this were the case, then church buildings would never have to be paid off, collections would never have to be taken up (except by those with the gift), and missionaries would never have to ask for funding. Giving today is non-miraculous.

Perhaps you've known folks as I have who give big. Always giving. Need arises? They give, and give big. They still have to hold a job and work, but they never seem to run out or run short of money. To begin with, they have the native ability to give: fear doesn't get them- and neither does pride! God has his hand in there, too. No matter what they give, he gives back in the form of pay raises, tax breaks, 'luck' in the stock market and a big boost in their 401K somewhere along the way from the corporation. Hmm, reminds me of a promise that God made all of us in Second Corinthians chapters 8 and 9, but for another time. But lest I leave you with the dollar for dollar match guarantee from God, let me also say that the giver might give a dollar--and get back 50¢ and a friend!

The mercy givers are the ones who captivate my attention. Usually quiet. Usually not up front pounding the pulpit or out front leading the church family through thick and thin. They may not be teachers, leading young minds and old in the ways of the Lord. They are probably not the five talent Christian, who is the first in line to show the Master that the money was doubled, exclaiming, "See, I have gained five more talents!" They are the wildcards that get you back to sea when your life has run aground- or you have driven your boat onto the rocks of your own doing and now are in danger of capsizing, spilling all into the ocean of distress.

You know the drill. You screwed up royally in life. You attempted to hide it but that was paramount to sending up flares in the night. You denied it. You wrestled with it. You came to the realization that you will lose. You are repentant, but ashamed. You walk into the church building with the tips of your ears already red and hot. You are on the defensive for anyone who would extend an accusative finger. You lay it out and expect the worst. Someone gasps. Others shake their heads. Some look down and won't look at you. Some offer condolences and speak in generalities and say things like, "We love you" or "God will forgive you." Many walk by. Some shake your hand and mumble something you can't make out while they stare at the floor. No matter who says what, you feel like a total heel and a total stranger to the family you love.

Perhaps not there, maybe the next day, you come in contact with the mercy giver. You don't really know this person other than the face. You have never really talked with them before, except to ask them to serve on a committee in the past. You pause and talk now--they listen. They don't rake you or offer you advice. They don't accuse you or offer you a program or a book to read. They are just there, listening. But it is an active listening. As you speak, it is as if your very heart is being filtered through them somehow and coming back to you with far fewer impurities than it went out with.

Your conversation and encounter with them is through. You feel better. Not simply from a cathartic point of view by simply getting something off your chest. No, you feel as if this person actually accelerated the healing process. In short, you were shown mercy. The same type of mercy that the Father gives.

Is mercy giving a body gift, for the building up of the saints in love? You decide.

Let's take the time to quickly review what we have discussed thus far, before we close here and enter the allelon (One Another) section:

1. Our vertical relationship with God is directly proportional to our horizontal relationship with each other in God's family. The horizontal defines the vertical.

2. As disciples of Christ, we are uniquely qualified to both share in salvation and work within the church. The latter is called Body Life.

3. God never meant his church to be a place. Always a people. Always.

4. Within the church, we are called to work for, and with, one another under the umbrella of love. This is the only way folks will truly know we are His.

5. God never asks us to do what he will not empower us to do. We are equipped to carry out Body Life through Ministry Giftedness, according to our ability.

But how does one discover just what their Ministry Giftedness is? Is there some sort of test that will help one figure out just what they are gifted in? Answer: Lots of tests. Hit any church growth outfit, or pick up any church growth book, or visit any www.com after you Googled CHURCH GROWTH and chances are you will find the names of folks and businesses and seminars that will help one discover what their area of giftedness is. Being outside the scope of this book, I will simply reiterate some guidelines about Ministry Giftedness:

1. Each disciple of Jesus is given a gift or gifts according to their ability.

2. Spiritual gifts are not native ability, even though this in and of itself is from God.

3. Spiritual giftedness will be tied to native ability. Spiritual giftedness discovery may be found through preference (because preference reflects, by and large, native ability).

4. The only test for giftedness is through controlled trial and error coupled with prayer (lots of), always taking advantage of the open doors that God provides.

5. Spiritual giftedness does not preclude responsibility in other areas of our Christian walk. If it is in the Bible, it is our responsibility.

6. Gifts are given for a reason, and that reason is Body Life. Never for self glorification.

God went before the Israelites in a fiery pillar by night and a cloud by day as they left Egypt. He went before them throughout the land of Canaan like a stinging hornet. God was prayed to in Acts 4 to do the same.

We don't need a pillar of fire, cloud or a horde of stinging hornets. For sure, THAT would be the bee's knees, but we don't need it. We receive our Helper to dwell in us, to work through us, to lead us and to empower us with Ministry Giftedness to carry out Body Life--the greatest power that the world has ever seen. Before we receive that Helper, we can be talented, smart, outgoing, friendly, good looking, and a half dozen other things that God doesn't care about in and of themselves. It is when we choose to be led by that Helper that we will find ourselves backed by God, blessed by God and rise to do things that we never thought possible.

If this is not our experience, the answer is not, "God doesn't work in folks today" but rather, "We have not allowed God or sought God hard enough to lead our lives." Consider some brothers and sisters I have known over the years. I believe these folks were exercising their spiritual giftedness. They may not have recognized such, indeed some of them looked confused when I began to talk to them about it, but they were exercising it nonetheless.

Sister #1-Quiet. Back row person. Not a big conversationalist. Indeed, would hardly look you in the eye when she was talking with you. Taught children's classes some, but they weren't anything that the kids really carried on about. Worked as a period costumed person in one of those vacation places, but always in the background. Not a public speaker. But she was an encourager. She knew just when to send a card to someone. More importantly, she knew just what to write in that card to lift your spirits for a long time after that. It was evident that this sister kept connected to God through prayer. I personally have a card that I have kept for almost twenty years now. I know where it is and pull it out when needed.

Brother #1-Successful businessman. Midas touch. PhD

in Business Analysis. Couldn't really carry on a conversation with common folks like you and me for his comments were way too much over our heads. Lone Wolf in the body. But he was a teacher of little children. Each time it was announced that the children were dismissed for the Children's Hour, the kids tore out of the sanctuary like it was on fire. They always came back talking about this and that subject and what they had learned that day.

Brother #2-Low self esteem. Quiet. Hoping to never get involved in public worship. If he saw the 'worship coordinator' coming, he would freeze like a deer in the headlights. With much coaxing, akin to putting a cat in a paper sack, this brother sat through a 'Men's Training for Worship' class. After studying the lessons for prayer, he agreed to lead a prayer 'just once.' Turns out, he was a prayer warrior. When this brother prayed, you knew you were in the throne room of God.

Sister #2-Simple person with a hard life history. Not much in the way of interaction. Rather sit back and listen than get involved in conversation. Not outgoing and never going to get involved in active evangelism. She was a server. What kind? Can serve the entire congregation in get togethers--cook for 145 people, serve and clean up and love every minute of it- and make everyone helping her love it! Beyond that, anyone (sisters, and brothers!) who worked with this sister on these occasions enjoyed themselves instead of being stressed to the breaking point as is often the case. This sister being a new convert herself, would often find herself paired with other new converts (courtesy of the leadership) in a front line effort to expose them to Body Life. When one was paired with this sister, they felt needed and important. They would tie themselves into Body Life.

Sister #3-Quiet. Not sociable by the world's standards. Wasn't about to speak up or out concerning the Word of God. Though she never hosted the body in her house, she had a gift for setting up numerous small group and individual evangelistic Bible studies. Though she never taught directly, she brought enough folks to the Lord to start a large adult Sunday school class. In all, she was directly responsible for about 28 conversions in half that many years--all came through her personally. She never taught. She always sat there quietly. She was an Andrew [3]. She was a preacher's best friend. She lives a half a continent away and I wish she lived next door.

The list could go on. We can attribute this to luck, age, hidden talents or sheer determination. Question-what is the logical attribution? Are we not the children of the God who is able to do exceeding abundantly beyond all that we ask or think, according to the power that works within us? A little personal belief about luck. If you believe yourself to be having a 'lucky streak' in your Christian life (which is your everyday life, not just Sunday morning), then next time you 'hit it big' or 'luckily stumble into' something, then attribute it to Lady Luck or the Luck of the Draw (or your good looks or dashing personality) and watch it wither on the vine. There is no lucky streak, lady or not, for the Christian. There is, however, a God on the throne...

Oftentimes, preachers, pastors, shepherds and elders try to fit all folks into a box that the Bible knows nothing about. This oftentimes comes in the form of a program aimed towards outreach and evangelism. This is usually tied to the fact that the leaders have been number crunching, either on the tithing, contribution or the attendance, and found a deficit. Since Christianity is a race, we ought to think of ourselves as a racing team. On that team there are pit workers. Off the track there are mechanics. There are promoters and bean counters. There's a secretary and a promoter somewhere. Only one drives the car across the finish line and gets the roses. All win. We're not all race drivers (or bean counters), nor can we be. It takes everyone.

One last item before we move on. It is pride. The proverbial writer put it plain and simple in Proverbs 16:18 when he wrote, "Pride goes before destruction, and a haughty spirit before stumbling." Pride needs to go in the same roundfile as Lady Luck. No pride--for it takes all of us as different body parts. Paul spoke of it in First Corinthians 12:12-18 when he spoke of the body of Christ being like the human body: one body part can't say it has no use for another body part.

One of my instructors, Abe Lincoln, had something to say about body parts and pride. He quite frankly said that he didn't "...care if you were an eyeball as big as Dallas and could see all the way to Amarillo--if you didn't have any feet, you simply weren't going to get there!"

Actually, he had quite a few sayings like that. He's currently on the other side of the Jordan and, I'm quite sure, entertaining the troops with some such sayings.

Paul finished his illustration of body parts, and the functioning thereof, with a simple statement that we would all do well to pay attention to: "But now God has placed the members, each one of them, in the body, just as He desired." If Paul were speaking of the church local (and he was writing to the church local), one's head should spin at the ramifications of such a statement. Did God specifically place that teen or that elderly couple in your particular congregation instead of the one three miles or three blocks away? Again, what is the logical conclusion?

One begins to see where the idea of Body Life and Ministry Giftedness leads. It leads to Allelon--One Another.

Questions for thought or discussion:

1. Discuss the fact that every disciple is God gifted from their conversion.

2. Do you know what your gifts are? List what you believe your gifts to be.

3. Would God gift each and every one of us without a reason? What do you believe that reason is?

4. Does God work through His people today (as in really or literally)? How is this done? Can you think of an example in your life?

5. What does the phrase in Romans 12:3 "as God has allotted to each a measure of faith" mean to you?

6. What was the slave in the parables of the money usage (Luke 19 & Matt 25) judged harshly for? Did the master in the story (our God) need the money that badly? How can this parable be reenacted today?

Endnotes:

[2] Some may be asking, "What in the world are you talking about?!?" In my particular flavor of church growing up, it wasn't uncommon for someone to lead a prayer right before the Preacher preached. The prayer offerer would ask of God to, "Give the one who speaks to us this morning a ready recollection of the things which he hath prepared." The prayer man may not have fully understood, but he was asking God to dip into the Preacher's mind and remind him. He was praying for short term, on the spot inspiration for the Minister.

[3] Taken from the story found in John chapter 1. Andrew took his older brother to go see Jesus. An Andrew is someone who doesn't teach, but rather takes the seeker to someone who can.

The Body: Harmony & Peace

We are members of one another and, therefore, are mandated to live in peace and harmony with one another. If mandated to live this way, we must pursue, not hinder, these one another commands.

Ah, family vacations! A family of five takes off from Arizona at the same time a family of four takes off from Colorado. Both will arrive at their destinations about the same time, if they encounter no problems along the way. If the weather holds with no sudden downpours and the children do not make too many demands about stopping here and there for trinkets and junk, the two families will make good time.

Meanwhile in St. Louis, a childless couple by choice are making last minute preparations to board a plane in less than six hours. There are plants to water and dogs to board. If the flight doesn't turn into a disaster due to diversions, circling or they have to contend with lost luggage, they should make their destination late that night. In a few other parts of the country, people began to stir much in the same manner. All are being pulled to the same location.

They're all headed to north central Texas. All headed to the same town, the same street and the same house. It's family reunion time! All total there will be Great Grampa, Regular Grandma and Grampa, four adult children plus spouses dragging along a total of 8 kids of mixed sexes ranging from 18 down to 1/2. Toss in a Cousin Ernie who one "hasta watch kinda close on a few things" and you have the makings for a fun filled week at Reunion City.

Now unless you are too young to have had much of life's responsibilities or you are an only child who was kept in the attic, you are cringing right about now and relieved that it isn't you that is having to host or otherwise attend this extravaganza. The younger teens don't want to be seen anywhere in the vicinity of the older folks (of 28 years of age on up). The babies want to cry, eat and nap. Great Grampa wants to nap. Aunt Mabel wants to tell about her gallstones and Cousin Ernie wants to...well, never mind what Cousin Ernie wants to do.

Do we not like to see one another? Of course we do, but we're no dummies. Holding a family together of three to six or whatever under one roof on a daily basis is hard enough work at times. Holding an extended family of a dozen and a half together for a week without someone going to jail or the morgue is even harder work! What on earth makes us think that we can gather 45 to 400 to 1200 folks together for a church family, make them physically come together three or more times a week without someone either going to jail or the morgue before we finish the invitation song, and not put a drop of work into it?

But we try it all the time.

How many of us parents have bellered that we want peace and quiet in the house from time to time? Peace is the absence of open conflict, sometimes with small arms or swords or clubs. Quiet!--as in peace and quiet, is the absence of unnecessary noise. This may be carried out through separation into bedrooms, or redirecting the smaller occupants of the house to engage in something together with a common goal: Monopoly, Sorry, or building a Lincoln Log house. This latter is harmony.

At the end of Mark chapter 9, Jesus makes a very short but bold statement: "Be at peace with one another." He was looking ahead to his church and knew, what we all know, that the world would take one look at a fighting gaggle of people and decide right then and there, without any further investigation, that they simply would not want to be a part of anything like that! The fighting gaggle church can stand there and proclaim all they want about "We have the correct doctrine!" to lost folks, but those lost folks simply will turn away from the fighting and noise. The church is to be the escape hatch from the world. When the hatch is opened and the desperate crawl through, if the scene isn't different the desperate will simply back up, out, and reseal the hatch.

In desperate times, misery doesn't necessarily need company.

Consider a small church in Texas. On any given Sunday morning the attendance would be 57. Not 55 or 56. Not even 58, except for major traveling holidays. It was 57 on Sunday mornings. The small church was located in a small town. As with many small towns and churches, there tended to be quite a number of folks counted among the saints who were related to one another. Common great-great-grandfather who carved out the first 640 acres of land. Fourth cousins and other folks tied together by marriage. Initially, it looks good to the bustled, crowded up Christians in the larger cities. I've talked to numerous saints in larger churches of 700 or 1600 who pine and long for a smaller church where 'everybody knows your name.' Well, hang on to that thought. The fifty seven member church rocked along, until someone pulled out the Big E.

This is the word that causes all saints to freeze like rabbits on the roadway. At other times, it is akin to shouting 'fire!' in a crowded theater or yelling, 'she's got chocolate!' at a Lamaze birthing class. The Big E causes saints to dig in like a hound that doesn't want to go outside in the rain, or behave like a cat who doesn't particularly want a bath that day, bubbles or not. What is the Big E?

Evangelism!

But this was a different type of evangelism than the cold door knocking or doorknob hangers. This was the type of outreach that sought out and went after folks who had previously been associated with that particular church family in years past. That's when the real trouble started. The comments went something like this:

"We all understand what you are trying to accomplish here. Probably a good thing, but we're under the impression that you should let sleeping dogs do just that."

Or, "They left for a reason, and that reason ought to be good enough for all of us."

Or, "If that side of the family starts coming here, I'm outta here."

Or, "They can come back if they like. It's a free country. But don't expect me to be all huggy huggy with them. We have a long, looonng history Pastor, that you couldn't even begin to understand."

By now you've guessed it. The goners and the stayers were all part of a physical extended family! They were nowhere near living at peace with one another either inside or outside the church building. Worse, they had all made up their minds long before any preacher suggested the Big E that they were not even going to attempt to reconcile whatever it was that tore them apart in the first place, and live in peace. No, they opted to live in pieces.

All across this country, a significant number of church buildings stand empty, or nearly so, because the occupants decided to forgo one or more of Jesus' one another, or allelon, commands. They opted to nurture and grow their petty differences for the sake of the fight instead of living with one another in peace. We're geared for the fight. Our society gears us for the fight. The letter in the mailbox from the city zoning. The letter from a lawyer's office. The phone rings and Caller ID tells you it is long distance and you don't recognize the number. A message from your child's teacher that asks you to return her call. You stop and examine the new cars on the lot and a salesman approaches. You arrive at the church building on Sunday morning and a family you've never seen is sitting in your pew...

Topping the list of the greatest fears in modern medicine is one of rejection. This is the fear of any organ transplant or any operation that attempts to reattach a severed arm, finger or toe. A shepherd in my preaching career that I've had the highest respect for, even to this day, had once gone through a kidney transplant many moons before I ever met him. One of the things that was always forefront in his mind was kidney rejection, even after many years.

What a trauma that must be to have the body either attempt to reject something new (or at least new to that body), or attempt to reject something that was there, left, and then returned. So, we get the picture, right?

We will try anything to keep the reattached limb or new liver. We strengthen the other body parts. We will watch with diligence any and everything that is ingested into our body. We get extra rest. We watch our weight. We read and read and read to arm ourselves with anything that will give us just a little more of an edge in keeping rejection at bay. We will even listen to great Aunt Mabel's home remedies for keeping newly transplanted lungs.

In the Kingdom of God, folks are being transplanted in. Paul discussed this idea with the Roman church, but called it being grafted onto the tree. Sometimes folks are reattached after being severed. Jesus called this the lost coin, lost sheep or the lost son in Luke chapter 15. Living in peace with one another, living in harmony with one another, or being of the same mind toward one another would demand all the attention that we would give a reattached big toe or a donated heart. Our empty pews and outdated church directories speak more of toe*nails* and heart*burn*.

Centuries ago, it was proposed by a few that the earth was not the center of the universe. This caused quite a tiff in religious circles. This also caused quite a number of folks to be thrown into prison and burned at the stake. It didn't seem right. Sun comes up on our right and down on the left at night. Moon follows. The pattern seemed to indicate that we were on center stage. Finally, everyone figured it out. Books had to be rewritten and sermons had to be changed.

It is probably a merciful thing that we cannot remember the exact moment and circumstance when we learned that we, individually, were not the center of the universe or most important person at hand. For a while it seemed like we were. Uncomfortable? On empty? Cry!-and two faces would magically appear over our cribs. Worked up to a point and then we learned.

Some little shred goes with us into adulthood. It surfaces from time to time in family matters, at work and in our leisure time. We don't get our way or our suggestion was laughed at or we didn't achieve at something or a host of other situations. If unchecked, we will be written off in the adult world as a whiner, a complainer, a selfish person or other adjectives that denote an egocentric [4] person--and we will be avoided. Carry this into the church family, and there will be more than physical disappointments and undone work. When anything is brought into the spiritual realm, it will reap spiritual consequences--good or bad. When the physical body doesn't want to share nutrients and blood with a Johnny-come-lately heart or big toe, soon the big toe ends up shriveled in the bottom of the boot when the foot is pulled out. It becomes very difficult to walk. When the physical body rejects the heart, the doors are closed.

"But I don't want to make peace or live in harmony with some of my brethren. You don't know the half of what my family has been through with some of these people. Can't I just ask to be in a different cell group than these people and say that I'll sit on the east side of the sanctuary and let those people sit on the west?"

Of course you can ask it and say it. One can ask and say anything, but that doesn't make for the fulfilling of a Bible mandate. Come down off of it and pursue peace and harmony with your brothers and sisters.

What is at stake if some in the church don't pursue the things which make for peace? What is at stake if we don't live in harmony with one another? For that answer, I take you back to the only sign that Jesus authorized to identify his people, found in John chapter 13, and that is the sign of love for one another as he loved us. I also ask that you consider two verses: Romans 14:19 and Philippians 4:2. First, Romans: *So then let us pursue the things which make for peace and the building up of one another*. Rom 14:19. There are several things about this verse that ought to stand out when we read it. First, the sentence is a conclusion *("So then"--never, never start a study with the words so then or therefore. Back up! Back up! Back up!).*

The second is that there are two items that the apostle wants each and every Christian to pursue with equal endeavor. Let's begin by examining the conclusion.

The large block of Scripture that begins in Romans 14:1 and continues well into chapter 15 (at least through verse 8!) concern themselves with weak and strong disciples. Not more saved or less saved disciples, just strong and weak. Some have concluded that the weak disciples were the Christians with Jewish backgrounds who couldn't let go of the Jewish food laws. Others have surmised that the weak were actually the new Christians out of a pagan setting who were confused by the freedom in Christ to eat anything and the allegiance shown pagan idols when that meat was consumed. Some see the strong as strong headed. Either way (you decide after studying the passage), Paul tells them that all who belong to Christ are in Christ and not barely in Christ. His final conclusion states emphatically that no Christian is an island, all should be convinced in their own mind of the things they feel they have to do, and we all have the mandate to lift up, not tear down.

His midway conclusion in Romans 14:19 tells us that we have a common pursuit: peace and building each other up. That little word *and* carries quite a bit of weight. It is just as important as Jesus' directive toward the end of the Beatitudes when he said of persecution coming our way, "Rejoice *and* be glad." Peter had just as much emphasis when he said, "Repent *and* be baptized." In the former, rejoicing is the action while being glad is the attitude. Attitude with no outward sign does little good, while the outward sign with no heart in it is simply an outward sign. In a similar way, baptizing a person who has not repented is simply a quick dip in the pool while repentance without immersion to reenact the death, burial and resurrection of Jesus falls far short of obedience.

In other words for our Romans passage, peace builds up the brethren. The brethren can't be built up without peace. One can teach all the Sunday schools in the world and preach fifty minute sermons complete with pulpit pounding, props and seventy-eight Bible references, but if the church family isn't pursuing peace, the church will not build. I believe this is what Paul had in mind when he wrote a certain church in Macedonia:

I urge Euodia and I urge Syntyche to live in harmony in the Lord. Phil 4:2.

Two sisters. Two women who wouldn't speak to each other. Two cats tied in a gunny sack. Two women who went out of their way to hurt each other by dropping hints and lines here and there among the rest of the church. Two women who had been like two peas in a pod, now as far as east and west. Two women whose Body Life had vaporized like the morning mist. Two women who stopped the ball of evangelism by dropping a one another command to live in peace and be of the same mind toward one another. What did they do?

I don't know. Through silence, Paul said it's not important. I'm sure some in Philippi knew. If they didn't know, it was none of their business. If the circular letter theory is true (*cf* Cols 4:16; I Thess 5:27), then it wasn't any one else's business, either. It isn't our business today. We don't need the specifics. We live out the specifics every day across the world. Euodia and Syntyche are countless brothers and sisters and families and whole families of God across town. It is the family that withdraws membership to go to another church building. It is the elder who steps down and steps out. It is the two sisters who haven't spoken to each other in months or years. It is the lack of peace that is passed to children who take up the banner for the sake of the earthly family honor. It is the five families that announce their departure from a local church congregation, only to go down the block and hang another shingle.

No peace, no sign. No harmony, no John 13:35. No like mindedness, no growth--however one cares to count growth. The right practice can be held on any given Sunday. The right interpretation of Scripture can be held. We can edit our song books to weed out the theological garbage (snappy tune or not). We can say all the right things around the communion table. We can use the right phrases in our prayers. We can place 110% of our attention to the vertical, but if the horizontal is not attended to, we have no ladder to climb.

We are members of one another and, therefore, are mandated to live in peace and harmony. If mandated to live this way, we must pursue, not hinder, these one another commands.

Questions for thought or discussion:

1. What does living in harmony mean to you? Does it mean the same as living in peace? What Scriptures did you use?

Allelon: One Another

2. List five words or behaviors you generally associate with helping disciples to live in harmony and peace.

3. List five words or behaviors you generally associate with hindering disciples to live in harmony and peace.

4. Think back to the worst incident of the breaking of harmony and peace within your church family. In the light of this section, how could it have been avoided?

5. How will you be able to assist your spiritual family to obtain peace and harmony?

Endnotes:

[4] Egocentric is just a fancy term for "It revolves around ME!" One of my favorite Beatles songs, written by George, is a song called 'I, Me, Mine.' Words go something like: No-one's frightened of playing it, Ev'ry one's saying it, Flowing more freely than wine, All thru' Your life-- I, me, mine. Talk about a snappy chorus! We really do need to get over ourselves and focus a little more on others.

The Body: Encouraging, Teaching, Admonishing, Confessing & Prayer

We are members of one another and, therefore, mandated to teach and encourage one another with admonition, confession and prayer. If mandated to live this way, we must pursue, not hinder these one another commands.

The last section on harmony and peace can just almost be pulled off without everyone knowing everyone. To put it simply, it is awfully hard to be at odds with someone you don't know. Awfully hard to be out of harmony with someone whom you don't know, perhaps, not even their name. But still, it doesn't make for a working model, especially of the church. Let's begin this section by examining what being open involves and, just as importantly, what it doesn't involve.

"Drop the masks. Be a transparent people. If you did it, let others know about it. Don't hold anything back. Come clean and you will be clean." All of us have heard these exhortations from the pulpit, religious periodicals and books to one degree or another. It's all, hopefully, under the heading of dropping the showcase and allowing the body to find a common place to begin to work in and with. It is also a fight against a basic survival instinct brought about by a common human gene we all share. Anthropologists, medical researchers and behavioral psychologists all identified this gene, and it is known as the 'I'm fine!' gene.

The gene [5] by and large, will lay dormant (switched off) until physiological stresses wake it up (switched on) so to speak. When the gene is activated (and I'm fast exiting my expertise here), it sends a hormonal response to the

47

hypoplasmian lobe of the brain via the pitaxiary gland. Once activated, it manifests itself in the human body by beginning to build a wall around us much as a slug, when bothered by salt or an eight year old boy, will begin to ooze slime for protection. What wakes (switches on) the 'I'm fine!' gene up from its sleep? It is activated when the brain perceives that we have come into contact with someone we do not know. Our level of acquaintance with that person is inversely proportional to the height of the wall the gene will throw up.

We shouldn't be shocked. We see this every day. I could get up in the evening (yes, was one of those folks that worked at night) and my wife would ask me (after coffee, of course) how I'm doing. I might reply that I'm currently OK, or I might (as usual) let her know that my feet hurt really bad that evening, and that I didn't get all the sleep I thought I needed that day. I'll offer that I hope tonight is a good one, but I'll reserve that judgment till after the 9 p.m. meeting. I may top that off by hoping that our weekend at Cousin Ernie's will probably make up for any undesirable things that may come our way.

I finally arrive at the hospital laboratory, after a ride where I've laughed at the bumper stickers and vanity plates and bemoaned a half dozen drivers. As I snake my way through the building, I'm asked the same question about my well-being by the first person I come into contact with. It may be the person I've seen at the hospital entrance nearly everyday for a year, but who works one floor above in a research something or other. It may be one of the secretaries or lab assistants we have floating around. It might be my boss or it might be the janitor leaving late. In each case my answer is the same as the gene kicks in its hormonal trip: "I'm fine!"

For lunch I travel down to the cafeteria, tuna in hand, to meet and eat with my friend, Duane, who happens to be in town again this week on a business trip and doesn't mind a midnight lunch. We went to college together and worked together for eight years until we were both laid off. I see him across the way and holler, "DooooWayne! Wassup?," to which he replies, "Nothing my brother from a different mother!" Then he asks me how I'm dooooin, to which I reply, "Well, if it weren't for these sore feet..."

Wait! What happened to those folks in my clinical lab when they asked me the same question that my wife and my bud asked me? Why didn't I give them the same response that I gave at home to my wife and at lunch with my best friend Duane? At this point, I'll dispense with the no-brainers and continue onto the two part dynamic at work here. 1- We don't want to tell these folks we aren't acquainted with every detail of our lives. 2- They don't want to hear it anyway! Now let's move away from the business world to the spiritual world and the folks known as the church.

I'm going to be just as honest as I can when I say that folks can get just a bit too open with each other for our collective good. If there does happen to be a book or a preacher out there who truly believes that we ought to tell every little deficit and sin and evil flash thought in our minds to the church, that author or preacher hasn't experienced the kind of Pandora's box that is created by pressing the issue.

In any church family, there are those who would run up and down the aisle on Sunday mornings and clot up the phones and stoops every night of the week with their problems and adventures. Histrionics, egocentrism, guilt-and other-complexes and a dose of narcissism are usually at work in these folks. Anyone who has hung out a shingle in the area of counseling knows this because they've experienced this with clients. To be sure, it speaks of instability in several areas of the person's life and is not necessarily related to a spiritual issue.

I'm not being cruel here or indifferent. We all have moments of anger every day. We all have wrong things we entertain every day. We all leave something good undone for any and various reasons. The Bible assures us of this. It is called humanity and can be found by way of example in the opening pages of every Bible. However, not everything (as in ev'ry li'l 'ol deet) was meant to be broadcast from the sinner's bench or the weekly church bulletin. How do I know this? I take my cue from Paul, who claimed to be the chief of sinners.

In Romans chapter 7, Paul tells us something we already experience with regularity: the things we know we should do we don't do, and the things we don't want to do (because they constitute sin) we do anyway. How messed up is that? And it comes one per customer whether we like it or not.

We're wretched people, and Paul reminds us by using himself as an example. What specifically was Paul into? None of your business or mine. If filling us in on the details of Paul's shortcomings were the right thing to do, we would know what it was. We would also know the identity of his thorn in the flesh mentioned in Second Corinthians. The Holy Spirit played a big hand in the writing of those two particular letters and saw the wisdom in leaving out the details.

With the sectional introduction out of the way, let's return to the hypothesis previous: 1- We don't want to tell folks we aren't acquainted with every detail of our lives. 2- They don't want to hear it anyway! At this point, let's not call it a hypothesis, but an axiom. It's been proven as a race of people, and in our individual lives as well. So, how are we to confess our sins one to another, pray for one another, encourage, teach and admonish one another if we do not know one another? Answer: we can't. Remedy for this section: get to know one another.

Again.......

How are we to confess our sins one to another, pray for one another, encourage, teach and admonish one another if we do not know one another? Answer: we can't. Remedy for this section: get to know one another.

Some church families do a great job at this. Some do a lousy job. Some think they're doing a great job but aren't getting the job done. Some leaders try and try but the family digs their heels in and refuses to do so. Where are you? I don't know, but it is hoped that you would pause for a moment and assess where your spiritual family is on this matter. Do you need small groups? Better managed Bible classes and studies? Small groups, perhaps? More get togethers? Small groups? Picture directories? Small groups? If it is lacking or ineffective, decide to be part of the solution instead of part of the continuing problem. What is at stake here? Everything this section is about.

Everyone ought to have someone they can talk to, confide

Understanding Body Life through the One Another Passages

in and confess their shortcomings and fears to. If this is not in place in your church family, it is not the fault of the preacher. It is not the fault of the elders. It is not the fault of the deacons, teachers, coordinators, and a host and list of other folks. It is a Whole Body shortcoming. All the aforementioned may hold their share of the blame, but it is a Body problem that needs Body attention. Plan to remedy this if there is no plan. Get a book, get a seminar, get a video series, get the pastor to preach a series on it, get an expert to come hold a meeting on it. Get going.

"But," you say, "I'm not the pastor!" The answer to that is, "Good, glad to hear that. He's busy with other things. This has been placed into your lap, so it's now your responsibility to get it going." Now, I do very much believe in spiritual leadership since it is very much a Bible topic. However, if your church is so tightly run that no disciple can practice Christianity without permission--then you're at the wrong place. Nuff said.

If we do not know one another; if we do not have someone to lean on in the body; if we do not feel comfortable enough to tell each other that our feet hurt--or we truly are having a great day, then all the encouraging, teaching, admonition and prayers will be greatly hindered to downright ineffective.

Out of our title list for this section, let's first consider prayers. I don't know you and you don't know me. I'm asked to pray for you because you're having a difficult time in your life. The request is generic--and the prayer will be, too. Remember that prayer is not for God but for the ones doing the praying. He doesn't need to be informed of our wants, lacks, and situations. After all, He is God and already has a handle on the news. Prayer helps us bend our will ever so closer to His. When praying one for another, we are helping hone and tune our hearts in the direction of that person who is the subject of the petition. Bottom line: do we care enough to stop and petition the God of the universe on this person's behalf?

For years, I kept an 'Emergency Prayer' in a little framed case behind glass. It hung on the wall with a little metal bar on a string next to it. The directions read "In case of emergency, break glass." The prayer read:

Allelon: One Another

> *"Dear Lord, we thankest Thee that Thou hast given us this opportunity to meet together to study another portion of Thy word. Be with the one who will speak this morning and give him a ready recollection of the things which he hast prepared. Forgive us of the sins of omission and commission--the things we've done and the things we want to do. Be with the missionaries the world over. Be with the widows and orphans. Help us to be a better friend and neighbor and if we've been found faithful, save us in the end. Guide, guard and direct us till the next appointed hour. Amen."*

For Pete's sake! All joking aside, this prayer smacks of not knowing the family or not knowing what is going on in that family. It is a prayer of distance and detachment. The one being prayed for is deflated. The family is not edified. All that was accomplished is a notch on a gun. One prayer--check! The vertical begins to crack.

After James tells us to pray for one another, he states that the effective prayer will bring about much. Much what? Much answers from God, but let's examine what kind of prayer is meant by an effective one.

The Greek word translated *effective* in the New American Standard and New International Version (KJV *effectual*) is *energeo*. We readily see our word *energy* in there, somewhere. Thayer's Greek Lexicon gives the number one entry definition *as to be operative, be at work, put forth power*. The word is used nineteen times in the New Testament, and translated *work* sixteen of those times! It is a quick, but correct, conclusion to state that the kind of prayer that James is talking about is a working prayer. A prayer that takes work from the righteous person.

A person who puts thought into the situation at hand. A person who carefully considers the request to pray. A person who takes what he knows about the will of God and bends the moment ever so much closer to that Supreme Will. That righteous person, when they get up off their knees, has done much to encourage the one who requested prayer.

The first area to bloom when one begins to open up and know his spiritual brothers and sisters is the area of encouragement. If there was ever a command with a built in warning, it is the one found in Hebrews:

But encourage one another day after day, as long as it is still called "Today," lest any one of you be hardened by the deceitfulness of sin. Heb 3:13

Again, what's at stake? The destiny of souls! Satan goes about like a roaring lion and we have the mandate to encourage. Now, words change meaning. For instance, a computer hacker today is a bad word. They create havoc and chaos, smashing into programs from a distance and corrupting them. Less than a half century ago, it was a person who took the initiative to dissemble a computer, figure it out, and write programs.

Encourage is one such word. It is the Greek word *parakaleo*, a compound word that literally meant to call alongside. In our postmodern day of shallow positive reinforcement, it has sadly taken on a different meaning. We regularly slap someone on the back and tell them to hang in there (I've heard that after someone responds to the invitation call and confesses their heart out--haven't you?), or tell them they're doing a fine job. While ministering full time, I began to experiment with trying to dislodge the backslapping that we've come to call encouragement. After the Sunday morning sermon, while standing in the back, I would shake hands with folks as they left the building. Some would say, "Preach, that was a fine lesson today." I would ask, "Which part did you particularly like?" As you guessed, the compliments stopped coming, and quickly!

This type of empty encouragement, when moved from a Minister's ego to a hurting disciple, is parallel to telling someone with a spiritual need to be warmed and be filled. It simply won't get the job done. It won't keep anyone from being hardened by the deceitfulness of sin. Notice other Bible passages that use the word parakaleo. Reading these will give us a deeper appreciation:

*Blessed are those who mourn, for they shall be **comforted**.* Matt 5:4

*And a leper came to Him, **beseeching** Him and falling on his knees before Him, and saying to Him, "If You are willing, You can make me clean."* Mark 1:40

*And they came to Bethsaida. And they brought a blind man to Him, and **entreated** Him to touch him.* Mark 8:22

*So with many other **exhortations** also he preached the gospel to the people.* Luke 3:18

*And with many other words he solemnly testified and kept on **exhorting** them, saying, "Be saved from this perverse generation!"* Acts 2:40

*Then when he had come and witnessed the grace of God, he rejoiced and began to **encourage** them all with resolute heart to remain true to the Lord.* Acts 11:23

*And they took away the boy alive, and were greatly **comforted**.* Acts 20:12

*I **urge** you therefore, brethren, by the mercies of God, to present your bodies a living and holy sacrifice, acceptable to God, which is your spiritual service of worship.* Rom 12:1

My apologies for so many quotations here, but enough to show that it's hardly a 'hang in there' kind of word. It is a word that is full of emotion and costs the encourager time. It is a word that demands we roll up our sleeves and be ready to dive into the deep end of the pool. It solicits our concentration and attention. It is synonymous with begging and pleading. It is work. It is a work that can neither be commenced or be completed without knowing who you are encouraging.

Please review that last sentence: It is a work that can neither be commenced or be completed without knowing who you are encouraging. We begin to get the idea that shaking hands with someone on Sunday morning will not get the job done. It is a place to start, but is not an end unto itself. That person that you are sitting behind on Sunday morning is someone that needs you--and you need them--in order to complete your journey with the Master and into Heaven itself.

Teaching and admonishing are one another mandates that, like encouragement and prayer, require a certain knowledge of the spiritual family just as they require a certain knowledge of God's will. "Nope," you say, "I've seen many an evangelist blow in, blow up and blow out and we didn't even know his first name. He certainly didn't know mine!" Wrong teaching, for we're not speaking of the pulpit preaching and Sunday school teaching--but the allelon teaching.

Let the word of Christ richly dwell within you, with all wisdom teaching and admonishing one another with psalms and hymns and spiritual songs, singing with thankfulness in your hearts to God. Cols 3:16

I'm not discounting the pulpit. There is a place for it, and it isn't a little place, either. I'll fight anyone who tries to remove the Sunday morning sermon, or to simply try and turn it into the Christian Happy Hour with props and histrionics. It is a place to be taken seriously, deadly serious, if the words of Paul to Timothy mean anything:

Pay close attention to yourself and to your teaching; persevere in these things; for as you do this you will insure salvation both for yourself and for those who hear you. 1Tim 4:16

It is my personal belief that the local minister should spend the majority, vast majority, of his time preparing the average two sermons and two classes that are given him each week. The pulpit isn't the place for a quickie or a gloss over--especially with the excuse that there isn't enough time to prepare a really deep sermon due to other duties such as blessing babies, announcing birthdays or other such cheerleading endeavors.

But we are all teachers. That we've seen in the mandates of teaching, encouraging and admonishing. Take the time to look up the remaining one another passages that concern themselves with teaching, admonishing and encouraging. Contextually, all will be commands for everyone and not the select few. Some will object, stating that they are not teachers. However, everyone is. We may be the wrong kind or even ineffectual, but we are teachers nonetheless. We teach through actions, words of conversation, lifestyle and the like. We give a sermon whether we like it or not, whether intended or not. But the Colossians 3:16 passage is, I believe, proactive. It is intentional teaching. Note the one another passage again, paying special attention to the prerequisites Paul places on the disciple before any teaching or admonishing will take place:

Let the word of Christ richly dwell within you, with all wisdom teaching and admonishing one another with psalms and hymns and spiritual songs, singing with thankfulness in your hearts to God.

Whole bunches of letting Christ in and through our lives and lots of wisdom precedes any interaction with one another in the area of instruction. So what do we teach? Easy, the Great Commission:

And Jesus came up and spoke to them, saying, "All authority has been given to Me in heaven and on earth. Go therefore and make disciples of all the nations, baptizing them in the name of the Father and the Son and the Holy Spirit, teaching them to observe all that I commanded you; and lo, I am with you always, even to the end of the age." **Matt 28:18ff**

At this point, I'm not talking about teaching on the upstream side of the cross. There is a place for this type of teaching, and just as ministry gifts do not absolve one of working in other areas, this section on teaching doesn't preclude evangelism. What we have historically lacked, however, is the teaching downstream of the cross. This is the "teaching them to observe" section of what Jesus commanded.

Notice that Jesus didn't say that we should simply teach them all that he commanded but to teach them to observe all that he commanded. Two words, one prepositional phrase, huge difference, great impact.

If we simply review Bible facts with one another without the application of Scripture, we will function little better than being an adult Bible Bowl. Nothing wrong with facts. David said he hid God's word in his heart so that he might not sin against God. That heart hiding started with facts, but went far beyond that to keep sin at a distance in the life of King David. No, King David wasn't pefect, but he was a man after God's own heart (*cf* Act 13:22 & I Sam 13:13*!*).

The type of teaching and admonition that is vastly needed in the body of Christ today, and every age, is one another-- one to another. It is life's experiences coupled with the word of God that need to be passed on to others. This principle is much in the same way as Paul's interpersonal advice to the church through his first letter to Timothy.

For example, many years ago a couple celebrated their 60th anniversary. Someone asked them to give the secret of their success. Being a youngster who was thinking of marriage at the time, I made sure I listened. We didn't get a "Put God first in your marriage," though that would have been a correct concept. We didn't get a "Always put your mate above yourself (Phil 2:3*f*)," which would have also been a correct concept. Instead, we got, "We never went to bed mad at each other, even if we had to sit up all night, plus we also always did the dishes together. This assured us of two things: no cockroaches, but also assured us of always doing something together every day."

Now at my young age, I had no concept of a married couple even remotely going to bed mad. I never thought of the importance of doing something together every day. I didn't know cockroaches. I've always remembered their words, though I can't remember their names. Being nearly four decades past, I'm sure they have gone home. But they taught, and it stuck.

I've already mentioned one elder who I especially hold in high regards. One day during my Minister tenure in the northwest, Ed came by my office, sat down and asked me how I was doing. Popped in out of the blue on his commute home from work. I began to reply what I was working on, how I thought this and that particular programs were going, what I expected to reap from another such program... He abruptly stopped me by waving his hand and restating, "I don't care about all that. I asked how you were doing." I was shocked! Anyone who has preached, pastored or ministered for any length of time knows from whence I speak--encouragement, teaching and admonition all rolled into one question! When the personal going gets tough, I often think back at Ed sitting across my desk, asking me that question.

If we cannot teach one another how to practically live our lives before God, then we have nothing to teach. I'm not advocating becoming the wise sage of the cave or the busybody of the brethren, but we must interact in such a way with each other as to bring the Bible's principles into everyday practice. Married folks, teach those who are dating what a Christian marriage is all about. Parents, teach the newlyweds what to expect when trying to raise kids in a Christian home. Widows and widowers, teach empty nesters what it will be like when one day they will be faced with leaning on God alone when that time comes and they are left howling like a wolf that lost his mate. Olders, teach youngers what it is like to weather the schemes of the Devil for five, six and seven decades--and to have sore feet.

We are members of one another and, therefore, mandated to teach and encourage one another with admonition, confession and prayer. If mandated to live this way, we must pursue, not hinder these one another commands.

Questions for thought or discussion:

1. Identify five ways you can encourage another disciple.

2. What are the differences between teaching and admonishing? Give examples.

3. Do you think disciples are reluctant to confess to each other? Why or why not? If not, what can specifically be done in your church family to alleviate this reluctance?

4. List five specific prayers you have prayed for another disciple. How did you view each of the people you prayed for afterwards?

5. List five items, actions, personality traits or situations that hinder biblical encouragement where you worship. What role can you play in curbing these hindrances?

Endnotes:

[5] Mapped out as the IAF76a gene on autosomal chromosome 13 by the Human Genome Project for all you biology buffs out there.

The Body: Forbearing, Forgiving, Comforting & Kindness

We are members of one another and, therefore, mandated to forbear and forgive each other through comforting ways while showing kindness. If mandated to live this way, we must pursue, not hinder these one another commands.

Forbearance must precede forgiveness. Without this precedence, forgiveness will oftentimes wind up as something less than forgiveness. We will fall prey to old adages such as "forgive and forget," which is humanly impossible. Without forbearance, we will be of little comfort to one another-- and kindness will be stretched out and out the window! Forbearance must be examined in light of the Scriptures. The two allelon passages are listed here:

*...with all humility and gentleness, with patience, showing **forbearance** to one another in love,...* Eph 4:2

*...**bearing** with one another, and forgiving each other, whoever has a complaint against anyone; just as the Lord forgave you, so also should you.* Cols 3:13

When the translators are faced with a Greek word that could be translated with several English words, they pick the one that would bring the most meaning contextually to the passage. Here are some other New Testament instances where the word translated forbear is translated differently:

*When we are reviled, we bless; when we are persecuted, we **endure**;* I Cor 4:12

*Therefore, we ourselves speak proudly of you... for your perseverance and faith in the midst of all your persecutions and afflictions which you **endure**.* IIThess 1:4

*For the time will come when they will not **endure** sound doctrine;* IITim 4:3

*But I urge you, brethren, **bear with** this word of exhortation, for I have written to you briefly.* Heb 13:22

But notice how it is translated in the gospels. All the same incidence, three different writers, all led by the Holy Spirit to capture what Jesus was both saying and feeling:

*And Jesus answered and said, "O unbelieving and perverted generation, how long shall I be with you? How long shall I **put up with you?** Bring him here to Me."* Matt 17:17

*And He answered them and said, "O unbelieving generation, how long shall I be with you? How long shall I **put up with you?** Bring him to Me!"* Mark 9:19

*And Jesus answered and said, "O unbelieving and perverted generation, how long shall I be with you, and **put up with you?** Bring your son here."* Luke 9:41

We don't use the word forbear, forbearance, forbearing. We use the phrase "put up with!" In order to connect and make our point, we will use it that way, too.

Allow me to belabor a point to make the last point clear about choosing words in translation. Compare Mark 3:21 and Second Corinthians 5:13. If you are reading the King James or the American Standard Version, the translators translated the root Greek word *existemi* as *beside himself* and *beside ourselves* respectfully (meaning off the rocker a bit). In the New International Version's rendering of Mark 3:21 it uses the phrase *out of his mind*, and the Second Corinthians citation as *out of our mind*. In the New American Standard Version, Mark is translated *lost his senses* and Second Corinthians as *beside ourselves*.

In Acts 2:7, in all four popular translations the Greek word *existemi* (a compound word literally meaning to stand outside of oneself) is translated as *amazed*. Amazing, isn't it? But it is an example that will allow us to use different words or phrases at times to translate a word, idea or phrase. Again, we don't forbear with folks in the 21st century--we put up with them... or at least God wants us to.

We're part of a family. Jesus set that idea in motion in Mark 3:34 when he said of the crowd assembled to hear Him teach, "Behold, My mother and My brothers!" when his physical family came to speak to him. On the one hand we are born into this spiritual family, as Jesus pointed out to Nicodemus in John chapter 3, and on the other hand we are, being wild olives, grafted into this family as Paul tells us in Romans chapter 11. In everyday, down to earth reality we are a bunch of different people who come from all walks of life, all colors, all educational backgrounds, all social backgrounds, all sizes, all shapes, all types of hyphenation, all ages and all of any thing else one wishes to make as a distinction.

We raise our children differently. We spend our money differently. We go to different movies and subscribe to different magazines. We drive different trucks and celebrate Christmas differently. We have different cellular plans and wear different clothes. Some keep their mustard in the icebox and some do not. Some like public schools for their children and some like private schools. Others think that home schooling is the only way to go. Some write checks for the contribution while others give cash only. Some read the King James only and mulch their grass. Others read the Revised Standard and bag their grass. Some will not shop where alcohol is sold and others will drink wine with their meal. Some of you carry your Bibles in those little padded, frilly zip-up carry cases--and some of us do not!

I could go on--and on, and on, but we get the picture. We've always gotten the picture. Even when we're not in the mood to look at a picture, this one won't go away not even for a day! I'm not like you and you aren't remotely like me, except that we breathe air and are called Christians. We're placed in the body of Christ and at times cry out (much like Jesus did when he descended the mount of transfiguration), "How long will I put up with you?!?"

Answer: how ever long we stay on this earth.

Putting up with the brethren is not the same as putting up with sin. Sin is sin and we have the heavenly mandate to put the broom up and lay the corner of the rug back down. There will be more on that towards the end, it being a one another responsibility in and of itself. We're talking about a host of things that come about in the normal course of human interaction ranging from little nuances to things that downright rub us the wrong way simply because we don't do them that way and don't have the same thoughts and ideas on the matter as others do ("Can you believe that she has the gall to wear white after Labor Day?").

Unless you came from a ravenously dysfunctional family setting, you've been faced with 'putting up with' others all your life. You've had to share a room, share clothes, watch stupid programs on TV because it wasn't your turn. You've entertained the baby and walked slow because Grandma is slow. You've had to quiet down because Daddy was on the phone and shown forced appreciation to Aunt Mabel for getting you that crochet starter kit on your 17th birthday. After your own personal trip down memory freeway complete with orange construction barrels, you know deep down inside you did it for the overall peace and harmony (remember those?) of the family. Why, at times, can't we seem to pull it off in the church family?

Sometimes we can't even pull it off for a couple of hours on any given Sunday in the church building, let alone our 24/7 calling for one another in the spiritual family setting known as the church. But we must, for the Master insists. This entire concept goes back to the getting to know one another spoken of previously. We know this to be true: it is much easier to put up with someone that we know as opposed to someone we just know their name--or not.

Returning to our earthly family, we put up with one another in the name of peace and harmony, yes, but we also do that in the name of maturity. Adults put up with children with the idea of maturity in mind. We know that they will (hopefully) grow up and grow out of their childish, often self serving, behavior. We gently remind them to stop talking back and to lower the tone of their voice, knowing that frustration and the inability to make good decisions is often behind their speech. We often close the door to their room instead of the constant battle to clean up, clean up! We know, that just as the tadpole loses its tail and becomes a beautiful toad, our children will lose their pig sty gene one day and clean it all up.

Children, depending on their age group, can show an amazing amount (to us adults, anyway) of forbearance with other children. They do it when they are entertaining the baby while we get supper ready. After canceling plans, they do it while entertaining their cousins when Aunt Mabel drops by unexpectedly. They are capable, at times, of sitting quietly in the back seat of the Rambler when we take those mega-mile vacations. However, they have their point of which they will endure no longer. We all do, but it is related to relative maturity. And so it should be in the church.

For examples in the church, let's go inside the church building for a Sunday morning worship or into a small group meeting in the back of that building on a Tuesday night. We know how hard it is inside a physical family to forbear, now let's examine the hundredfold mess that we can sometimes have on our hands, and why.

Everyone is present. Everyone is seated. Everyone is ready. Look around the room. Chances are you probably don't know everyone's name. Chances are all age groups are accounted for from oldsters down to newborns. There are relatively young folks who have been Christians for many years. There are old folks who have been Christians for many years. There are old folks who have been Christians for just a little while. There are some that have grown in the faith fast, while others seem content to stay in the spiritual crib. Trying to categorize everyone is a mind-boggling experience. To just say, "Everyone's the same," in reference not to salvation but to maturity is to join the ostrich examining sand grains. Knowing that God is blessing the time, never forget--almost like the cherry on top of our matrix--the one uninvited guest that keeps showing up wanting the whole thing to go away!

If you don't know who that one particular entity is, he is often described as wearing a red suit, pitchfork, and a red, pointy tail.

We begin. So far, so good. The redeemed have already sung *I'll Fly Away* and *Hilltops of Glory*, and boy howdy, did we sound good! Then it happens. Sister Rachel's kids begin to squirm. They begin to make noise. They begin to kick the pew in front of them. They begin to make lots of noise with their feet and their mouths. Sister Rachel is still singing *O Victory In Jesus* at the top of her lungs. She doesn't take them out. While the chorus before the communion is sung, everyone begins to make personal plans for Sister Rachel's children as the melody floats high above the sanctuary: *They are nailed to the cross, they are nailed to the cross...*

Brother Ralph and Sister Mabel have taken it upon themselves lately to be some sort of self styled greeters. It would be OK, except neither one of them can hear, and as with most nearly deaf folks they feel that everyone else is deaf, too. Long before Sister Rachel's kids started using the pew as a percussion instrument, Ralph and Mabel stood out in the foyer greeting the latecomers with a very loud, "Heidi-ho and how are we today?" Heidi-ho? What kind of holy kiss is that? And what's that 'we' stuff? Everyone in the worship gets greeted at least ten times with the very loud Heidi-ho. The only one who can possibly drown out the Heidi-ho is Brother Earl.

Brother Earl is the keeper of the King. The King James, that is. He insists on it to the point of becoming slightly angry. When he gets up to read a Scripture, he states very emphatically, "This mornings Scripture selection will be read from the King James Version of the Holy Bible." He sounds a bit like Alfred Hitchcock narrating a golf tournament. One would think that the small group study we have during the week would be a little more sane if it weren't for the M&M's.

It's not that Sister Julie insists on snacks. There's something about intensity that triggers her. There we are, the lesson has been presented and one of the brothers or sisters feels especially moved to talk about a shortcoming or burden in their life. The kind of sharing that requires a round of tissues to be handed out before the words can come out. That's when Julie springs into action. She steps into the kitchen and begins the search for the scissors. They're always in the same drawer, but she insists on rummaging through all of them. When the scissors are rounded up and the one pound bag of M&M's cut, then the noise: golf ball sized hailstones hitting a tin roof. We have plastic bowls, we have glass bowls, but she insists on a metal bowl--and pours from a height of two feet! As she enters back into the room, the room is a mess. Sisters are hugging sisters and telling them that they will be there for them. Men are sitting quietly and pondering what just happened. The air is one of forgiveness and healing. Sister Julie announces as she rolls the hailstones on the tin roof, "Anyone for M&M's?"

But that will be Tuesday night. We're not through here on Sunday morning yet. The song is over. The Heidi-ho's have taken their seat among the saved. The children are busy doing something and aren't kicking the pews anymore. Then Brother Earl grabs his King James Bible and mounts the podium...

I'm certainly not in favor of hosting Kids Gone Wild on Sunday morning. Neither am I in favor of the hosting of other disruptions that come our way when we are trying to each concentrate and reflect and examine. I understand distractions and truly believe them to be a tool of Satan. However, in our little snapshot of Anywhere, USA on any given Sunday, we saw no sin. We saw, to be sure, huge distractions, perhaps caused by poor choices and us not paying attention to how we affect others around us, but no official missing of the mark.

We get upset at the Sister Rachels. Perhaps she needs help with the kids. Perhaps she needs a close friend to help her and teach her at the same time. In the meantime, a whole lot of forbearance is in the forecast. Earl needs to be engaged in a conversation to see why he insists, and makes a point of his version, every time he gets up to read. The first and second answer you get won't be the meat of the matter. Ralph and Mabel don't need their enthusiasm squashed. They just might simply need someone to let them know that their voice carries. Anyone who can see through a ladder can see that Julie is bothered by sharing time. As a defensive mechanism, she will excuse and then disrupt. Something horrible has happened in her life and is now a thorn in her flesh. It's all about forbearance, coupled with teaching and interaction. One thing is for certain, if forbearance, or puttin' up with, is not exercised with these fellow disciples, there will not be an arena of forgiveness when the time comes. Pots will simmer and then boil over.

People will get mad. People will be hurt. People will leave. We have not traditionally recognized that people are leaving.

'Forgive and forget' is found in the Bible right next to the verse that tells us 'God helps those who help themselves.' Not knowing exactly where it came from, my best guess is from a misunderstanding of the figurative language God used when he says our sins would be remembered no more. He also said that they would be as far removed as east is from west. The wise guy quickly thinks about the other side of the world where east finally meets west, but it's figurative. He remembers them, but chooses not to count them against us. In fact it is impossible for God to forget things.

He remembered Adam and Eve's sin in the Garden of Eden. He remembered Cain killing Abel. He remembered Abraham saying of Sarah, "She is my sister!" He remembered all of these, and many more sins, since the Holy Spirit inspired the writing of Genesis. He wants us to remember the sins of the Hebrew slaves as they whined and built golden calves. He told us that through Paul in First Corinthians so we wouldn't do the same (even though we do). Jesus quite frankly stated in Luke chapter 17, "Remember Lot's wife." Remember what? The events and motivations in her life that caused her to be a permanent fixture on the plains: a real salty gal.

Even Jesus, to an extent, wants us to remember. One of his greatest teachings on 'getting things right with one another' begins by saying, "If therefore you are presenting your offering at the altar, and there remember that your brother has something against you..." We must remember--or forever be doomed to repeat and repeat and reap and reap. In the end, it's not whether God remembers or forgets that matters, it is what he chooses to do with it once it has been forgiven. It is the same with us today, for human forgiveness is to be like divine forgiveness in every aspect. Examine these two verses:

... bearing with one another, and forgiving each other, whoever has a complaint against anyone; just as the Lord forgave you, so also should you. Cols 3:13

And be kind to one another, tender-hearted, forgiving each other, just as God in Christ also has forgiven you. Eph 4:32

How should we do it? According to the Holy Spirit, we should forgive each other just as our Lord forgave us. I truly believe that this is one of the first areas that breaks down as we ever so slowly try to separate the vertical from the horizontal. We sing *Redeemed by the Blood of the Lamb* with gusto. Our pulpits ring out with the reiteration that we are a forgiven people. Our prayers thank God that we are forgiven and, therefore, a saved people. Jesus, and other writers, wanted to remind us that our forgiveness from Heaven is very much tied to our ability to forgive one another here on earth. Notice these key passages:

For if you forgive men for their transgressions, your heavenly Father will also forgive you. But if you do not forgive men, then your Father will not forgive your transgressions. Matt 6:14f

So speak and so act, as those who are to be judged by the law of liberty. For judgment will be merciless to one who has shown no mercy; mercy triumphs over judgment. Jas 2:12f

My favorite teaching on this subject is Jesus' parable of the Brain Dead Servant. Take the time to read Matthew 8:23-35. I don't know about you, but I wouldn't know a denarius from a talent from a farthing from a mina if someone dropped a couple of them in my stocking at Christmas. I speak bucks. I've seen a dollar, a five spot, a sawbuck, a Jackson. Pretty sure I've seen a fifty and maybe a C-note. I've not seen a million, but can at least grasp the idea. Now let's look again at the parable with OUR money and buying power inserted for ease. The Brain Dead Servant owed $1.7 million dollars. I don't know how he got there, he just did. We all know what it is like to rack up debt, not really know how we got there, and then wonder from whence it is all going to come. We've all looked out the back window hoping that sometime during the night a money tree suddenly sprang forth from the little patch of earth known as our backyard. We see the Brain Dead Servant begging for patience with a promise to pay back.

We're already told in verse 25 that he didn't have the means to repay. We know all too well the feeling of hopelessness he must have felt. He's simply bargaining for more time much like the Chaldeans were in Daniel [6]. He's begging. His wife and children are crying, because their futures are at stake. The king shows mercy. What?!?

Now how about *that* feeling? One point seven million dollars worth of debt flushed down the ol' first century toilet. All of the stress and anxiety that both he and his entire family were suffering were gone with a few words from the king. No more sleepless nights with his head in his hands while sitting at the kitchen table. No more loss of appetite as he choked back the tears of frustration. No more pounding headaches as he pounded his fist on the dashboard as he commuted to work each day, wondering what tomorrow would bring.

Before we go on to the rest of the story, it is always good to look back on our own lives. I think this, indeed, captures what Paul was asking us to do in First Corinthians chapter 11, oh, about verse 28. The big question is: what kind of feeling did you have the moment the God of the creation said to you, "Don't worry about it. I'll forgive your debt to me. Case closed?" But we return to the Brain Dead Servant.

Not one verse separates the next action. The recently forgiven slave, new lease on life, finds the first poor fool that owes him money and begins to choke him. Why? He wants the $400 bucks owed him. Wait! $400? --$400! He owed $1.7 million dollars to the king--four thousand, two hundred and fifty times more money than this poor chowderhead owes him! He wants $400 bucks! His buddies, for sure, cut a fast track back to the king. They couldn't wait to cash in on that one! The one moved with compassion in verse 27 is now, by verse 34, moved with anger. The slave of our story was simply unwilling to recreate the forgiveness shown him. He was unwilling to carry out in the horizontal that which he experienced in the vertical. It cost him. Not the $1.7 million dollars. It cost him...him.

We have this story as a reminder. Why we have this story is found in verse 23 as Jesus says, "For this reason." Peter thought he was doing well by forgiving someone seven times.

Allelon: One Another

At times we think we're doing someone a favor by forgiving them seven times. Not seven times in a day, but seven times in a lifetime. We figure that, based on being around someone an average of six years, we could forgive them on the average of every 10 months plus a week. That ought to be good enough, shouldn't it?

Only if that is how we wish to be treated by God. We don't.

God doesn't ignore our sins. Neither does he turn his head nor pretend he didn't see or hear anything. He doesn't excuse or say things like, "Well, that's just the way they are!" He doesn't pull up the end of the rug with broom in hand. However, he is in the forgiving business. Continually. God could have made any number of comments at the end of what we call the Lord's Prayer in Matthew chapter 6. He certainly covered a number of subjects in that prayer. What he did say was,"You forgive, I forgive. You don't, I don't."

A preacher search had been done in a medium sized congregation. It took over a year to find just the right man for the pastoring job, but it was finally over. The excitement had grown in the church with the prospect of once again getting back on track and moving forward after a year with a vacant slot. The new minister *et.al.* moves into town and many are there to help him move in and unpack. Folks make comments along the way that all add up to the fact that most programs had lagged, staggered and stagnated over the past year and all were ready to get going once again. One could almost see the heavens opened and hear an angelic choir in the background singing, *"To the work! To the work! We are children of God!"*

As any minister would do, he began to look over the church directory. He began to meet folks and learn names and pair them up in his mind. One afternoon he caught an especially vibrant and enthusiastic sister and asked her if she would be interested in working in a particular area. Her feet almost left the ground as she excitedly gave a resounding, "Yes!" She had some ideas on the matter and soon they were off and into a discussion of how to build this area from dream to reality.

Along the way, the preacher suggested that getting others involved soon would be the boon they needed. She agreed. She had some names and laid them out. He had one name and he offered that. The room got quiet and the temperature dropped. A story began to hatch.

The (not any more) enthusiastic sister's children had been playing with that other person's children and one child hit another and she knew they were small children but she suggested to that other person that she needed to keep her kids in line and that other person got all bent out of shape and said some things and when the (now very agitated, and not a drop of...) enthusiastic sister got home she told her husband and he called that other person's husband and the two families got mad and the then preacher got involved and things were said and it was a long story and the new preacher surely didn't want to hear it all.

He had one question. The answer to the question told him that this incident had happened twenty-three years earlier. Twenty-three years. Almost enough time to pay off a thirty year mortgage. Certainly enough time to conceive a child, raise him, college him and send him on his way! Enough time to grow a fir tree to full maturity. Enough time to go through 2.6 dogs. Enough time to forgive.

The conversation died with, "Well, you just don't understand." The enthusiasm for the work died and never resurrected. The growing bond between the preacher and the once enthusiastic sister peaked on that day and then began to slowly decay, never recreating itself. Other areas were affected, too. Still, the two sisters never budged. Unforgiveness is like that. It destroys far beyond the bounds that one would expect them to be contained in.

Satan will tell us to just to ignore it: "So what if two people or two families aren't speaking to each other. It's not that big a deal." However, it is.

When unforgiveness is allowed to reign and run rampant in a church family, at any level, the paint on our John 13:34 sign out front of the church building begins to crack and peel. Given enough time, the sign becomes illegible. It becomes open to interpretation as folks try to examine what was once written there. Soon, they won't even bother to slow down and attempt to read it. At that point, the Great Commission is out of commission.

If forgiveness isn't forgive & forget then what is it? As we have seen (and as we all well know) we're not going to forget that which has happened in our lives. God is not going to forget. He can't. He's the God of the universe. Just as we put forbearance into plain English, let's put forgiveness into plain language, too. Give it up and get over it.

No, I'm not being silly here. I said, "Get over it!"

Sounds harsh doesn't it? Get over it. But I think that it speaks to us in our time. Let go of it and give up all rights of resentment and action against that person. Imagine if the Lord were to keep on and keep on--for instance, when we do something and feel bad. For a while, like Jonah, we attempt to hide in the hull of a ship. It didn't work for him and doesn't for us. We're flushed out and face God. We shift from foot to foot trying to think of an excuse or reason. We soon exhaust all our reasons and ask for forgiveness. Just forgiveness, nothing more. He says, "Yes." A great weight is lifted.

Later, we see the Lord again. Maybe later that day, maybe the next. He reminds us of what he did for us, forgiving us and everything. We say thanks again. He tells us just how terrible we acted towards him, but he forgives us just the same. Even later, he brings it up again, letting us know just how bad we were and how much it took to forgive us. We nod our head. Weeks later, he is still dragging us back and forth through the sin, reminding us that we better be good because he is the one who holds to power of forgiveness in his hand. Months later, we're still reminded ...

Now we do that to one another, but thanks be to God that he doesn't do this to us. He forgives, and gives up all resentment. Did he forget? Hardly, but just as the father in the story of the prodigal son acted towards the returning boy (might be worth reading that little story here just because. It's found in Luke chapter 15), so our Heavenly Father gives up all right to drag us back and forth for all eternity through our muck. James T. Kirk thought space was the final frontier. We know that forgiveness is. For many, we don't need to worry about the seventy times seven. We're still working on the first seven with some folks.

Forgiveness doesn't mean to pretend something didn't happen. Like the forgetting aspect of forgiveness, this would simply cause more problems. There are consequences that go with sin. We know that. The Bible states that. What we need to come to grips with is that consequences (as we will see in the last section in detail) are a learning part of our Christian walk. In reality, it is a learning part of our everyday life. How many churches are polarized today because of unforgiveness and resentment? Everywhere that I have either preached or been associated with, there are families that will not speak to one another. They avoid by sitting on the opposite side of the auditorium. They avoid by avoiding the same small groups. They avoid by spending their time--no, wasting their time--finding out what program the other person is into so that they can bypass that one. It is a shame, and as noted, a waste of time and energy that could be better spent for the Master. So, how do we bring about genuine biblical forgiveness in our lives and the lives we touch?

To begin with, forbearance must be in place. Forbearance speaks of maturity and understanding. Forbearance is kind and not vindictive. That attitude must be present before any forgiveness can take place. Secondly, separation must cease and the situation must be confronted.

I don't want confrontation to be a bad word here. We often think of confrontation as solely taking place when one or more people get their tail feathers ruffed up and ready for the fight. No such thing intended here. We watch too much TV. It is simply the opposite of separation, but with a purpose.

Make no mistake about it. When we are sinned against, we will be hurt! We will feel bad and want to move away from the situation that always involves a person or two. Inanimate objects cannot sin against us- only people can pull that off. We want to back off to ease the hurt. We want to back off in order to not intensify the situation. We want to back off in order to protect others such as friends or our children. Backing off is a natural reaction. Staying off, however, is not. Satan loves it, but forgiveness cannot begin to grow in that type of an arena. When the initial hurt and shock are over, it is time for the confrontation.

Again, this is not coming at one another with pitchforks and torches. Save that for the monster movies. We are not monsters, but human beings with all the warts and scars that come from living on this planet earth. It is called confrontation because the situation needs confronting. As a counselor, I've seen many attempts to forgive, Bible style, thwarted because the two parties came together pretending that nothing happened. Something happened, and unless that something is attended to it erupts bigger and brighter in just a short while.

Talk about it. Assure that forgiveness is what is sought after. Use forbearance and kindness. Make it into a time of comfort for both parties. Promise to do whatever is in your power to make sure the sin is not recreated and repeated. Promise to give up resentment manifested by dropping little lines here and there to the brethren in our attempts to keep the offense alive. Promise to do one proactive item with that person in the near future, if possible. It might be as simple as a cup of coffee [7].

I said, if possible, on that last one. Many have jumped ahead of me into the worse kinds of sins that we can commit against one another: I steal from your house while you are away. I abduct one of your children and mess them up mentally for life. I shoot one of your family members or rape one of your relatives... The quick answer to all of that is you will not be able to work on one proactive item with that person unless you visit them at the prison on visiting day. This is why we have jails and prisons--for the disruptive and dangerous people inside the social network we call everyday life. If you shoot someone, you will go to prison, and probably be executed. Can you be forgiven? Yes. Can you get out of the consequences? No.

But that's not what is tearing our churches apart. We're not killing one another physically or stealing and robbing from one another (though James tells us we do this figuratively to one another). We're saying and doing things that go all the way from hurting one another to just simply rubbing each other the wrong way. And we quickly pick up and carry grudges for a long, long time. Satan is, I'm sure, upset that I'm letting his little secret out of the bag. Can two families in a tiff disrupt the church, even if the tiff contains no sin other than the sin of tiffing? It is my belief that we both know the answer to that question, and have seen the answer in real life.

We've already seen that it can squash a program and sit on evangelism. It can cause (and has) others to vacate the premises for other, any other, pastures because they simply can't take the attitude anymore. It will cause (and has) elders and deacons to step down from their work. It will cause (and has) pastors to once again pack up the U-haul truck for another work. Unforgiveness will cause preachers to open the ministry want-ads and begin looking elsewhere. It can cause (and has) teenagers, who do not yet have the maturity and the adult way of 'dealing' with things under their belts, to count the days when they can scramble away from the spiritual family for a more sane environment that we call the world. Whole families will do the 'church hop shuffle' much like a carnival cakewalk. Simple endeavors such as vacation Bible schools and potlucks turn into disasters. The church can still come together on Sunday mornings and sing *It Is Well With My Soul* and sound like an angelic choir. But the cracks in the vertical grow even wider.

Do we need to spend any time on kindness? Perhaps. Some will say that it is a fast disappearing item in our society. Other times, it comes from the strangest places. Instead of compiling verses about kindness coupled with a long discourse, allow me a story from a not-so-long-ago bus ride:

Same route: Albuquerque to Fort Worth. Same time: night. Layover: once again, in Amarillo. Young mother, perhaps only just into her mid-twenties, struggling with a herd of bags and two girls, three and three months. It was evident by her luggage that she was headed somewhere for a very long time.

I've had little kids. I've traveled with them. It isn't easy, even when things are going very well. For this mother, it wasn't. The baby was becoming fussy and the little three year old was waking up. I sat next to their little carved out corner, knowing there was a story that was to unfold.

"It's hard traveling with small children, isn't it?" I opened the door of conversation.

"Yes, we have a long way to go. Just left Albuquerque. What about you?"

We talked of Albuquerque--what we liked and didn't. I explained I worked with children for a living, trying to keep her at ease talking to a strange, funny walking man in his middle age. I offered the three year old some stick gum and she took two. I held the baby while Mom went to the restroom. She watched my bags and I made the same trip. I found rather quickly that they were 'going my way' but much further. Soon, it was time to board east. Mom had more luggage than she had hands.

"Let me help you with your stuff."

"Oh, no, I can get it." She tried, but she was simply reenacting her boarding in Albuquerque. Perhaps she had someone there to start her on her journey.

Perhaps she was trying to maintain composure and not impose on a cripple. She loaded up kids and a few bags hanging on her shoulders. I gathered up the rest and boarded the bus ahead of her, finding her a seat opposite of mine.

"Thank you, sir," as she put her two children into seats for the next five or so hours. Soon, all three were fast asleep. At four in the morning, all children should be asleep. So should their parents.

Quick stop in Wichita Falls. If one didn't eat in Amarillo, then this was it. Bus stops for fifteen minutes--and the bus driver will leave you if not back on the bus. I was hungry, no starved! I didn't want to get off the bus in Fort Worth and have my family change their schedule to feed a starving man. As we pulled into the stop, the three year old woke up.

"I'm hungry, Mama."

"I know you are. We'll get something to eat when we get to Houston."

"How long is that?!?" and there was distress in the little girl's voice.

I don't know what their story was. Was Mom running from someone or something? I didn't know. Was she lacking in the provision department for her two children, or was she simply on the bus out of distress and end-of-the-rope? It doesn't matter. What mattered was that there was a child, and she was hungry. Houston was an easy ten or twelve more hours away.

I could tell by the little girl's response to her mother's now lost explanation that this wasn't the first time the little girl had heard the pronouncement of no food on the near horizon. I pulled out a twenty.

"Please, take this and get your kids and yourself something to eat."

"Oh, we don't have any money. I can't pay you back."

I can't pay you back. I wonder how many times the Jewish carpenter has heard the same line from people... and wondered himself. "Naw, take it. This was free. The money fairy dropped this in my wallet back in Amarillo. I'll watch your kids. Better hurry."

Soon, milk and other bus-manageable foods appeared. The three year old wasted no time. Mom wasted no time, either. It was only after we pulled away that she remembered the change.

"Nope, don't need it back. Remember, that was free money from the money fairy."

She knew I was lying to her. She had learned long ago when her childhood ended that there were no fairies and no free money. "But you didn't get anything to eat. Do you want some of this?"

"Nope, I'm not hungry, just sleepy." I turned my head to the window, hoping that my stomach wouldn't growl loud enough for her to hear. I realized, maybe for the first time, that kindness doesn't correct the past. It simply makes the here and now right.

We are members of one another and, therefore, mandated to forbear and forgive each other through comforting ways while showing kindness. If mandated to live this way, we must pursue, not hinder these one another commands.

Allelon: One Another

Questions for thought or discussion:

1. Describe five behaviors you associate with one forbearing another. Did these examples take place in a church building or not?

2. What does forgiving someone mean? Give examples from your life, whether they are good or bad.

3. Does a disciple who has offended you have to ask for forgiveness before you forgive? In light of how we forgive, explain your answer.

4. Do you think it is possible for comforting one another and being kind to one another to be in conflict?

5. Consider forbearing, forgiving, comforting and kindness, and explain which you think is the most important. Which one are you quicker to exhibit in your life?

Endnotes:

[6] Daniel 2:1-13 is tragically funny. Imagine a bunch of conjurers dancing from one foot to the other with sweat pouring down their temples crying, "O king, live forever!" I'll just bet they were looking for the door with the bright red EXIT sign over it, also.

[7] I'm just sure that I read about coffee somewhere in the Bible. Pretty sure.

The Body: Being Servants, Submissive & Hospitable

We are members of one another and, therefore, mandated to be servants one to another showing submissiveness and hospitality. If mandated to live this way, we must pursue, not hinder these one another commands.

Something has shaped our idea of a servant. That something is probably Hollywood. When I was growing up in Oklahoma, there were plenty of folks around that could remember a time before moving pictures and, certainly, television. Their ideas, ideals and the little pictures we all get stuck in our heads were shaped by something else, but not the celluloid media. Today, that is simply not the case. The overwhelming vast majority of folks alive today are shaped by and large by television and movies.

The word servants will quickly conjure up scenes from *Birth of a Nation, Uncle Tom's Cabin, Gone with the Wind* and *Roots*. In fact, almost all discussions of servants, slavery and submissiveness will drift back into the slavery times in America. At least for a very long time, we will be fighting these images--and fight we must, for the biblical idea of servants was a far cry from our images.

In the first century, not all servants were unhappy. In fact, a vast number of servants chose to live that life with provisions being made in the Law of Moses (*cf* Exod 21). Unable to raise themselves up very far in their own family setting, some often chose to place themselves under others in exchange for a better life. At times, slaves were no different.

Slaves in the first century came about pretty much the way slaves do in every culture and every time zone: they were taken against their will. Many, after a time, were offered freedom. Many, like the voluntary servant, chose to stay right where they were, recognizing they had a better life than trying to return to the one they came from.

What was not all that uncommon during Roman times was for a slave or a servant to wind up as an adopted child into that family. Even adults were adopted. Upon adoption, all the rights and privileges of that family were transferred to the child or adult. No longer a slave, now a son (sound familiar?). A concept very nearly unheard of in the American history rendition of slavery.

There is more background material we have to fight in this country. It is the American Dream that goes well against the idea of being a servant but especially being submissive. The American dream goes something like this: let me drift across the Atlantic ocean on just a one gallon plastic jug. I'll go without food and water for days and months till I reach the shore. When I am finally washed up onto the eastern seaboard, I'll take my trusty pocketknife and, in no more than an afternoon, I'll jump into the pristine wilderness and carve out a thriving metropolis. In other words, New York City by four in the afternoon--and I'll get it done myself thank you very much.

We like Jesus as he is standing in the boat being the Master of the wind and waves. We cheer Jesus on when he is overturning the money changing tables in the temple. We nod and 'amen' him as he tells the Pharisees that they are blind guides and shout, "Hooray" when he finishes with those same Pharisees by calling them whitewashed tombs. We applaud his victory over death when he raises a little 12 year old girl out of death's grip. We are overcome when Jesus is victorious over his own death as the stone rolls away that quiet Sunday morning.

The enthusiasm slows a bit when we read these words found in Mark:

And James and John, the two sons of Zebedee, came up to Him, saying to Him, "Teacher, we want You to do for us whatever we ask of You." And He said to them, "What do you want Me to do for you?" And they said to Him, "Grant that we may sit in Your glory, one on Your right, and one on Your left." But Jesus said to them, "You do not know what you are asking for. Are you able to drink the cup that I drink, or to be baptized with the baptism with which I am baptized?" And they said to Him, "We are able." And Jesus said to them, "The cup that I drink you shall drink; and you shall be baptized with the baptism with which I am baptized. "But to sit on My right or on My left, this is not Mine to give; but it is for those for whom it has been prepared." And hearing this, the ten began to feel indignant with James and John. And calling them to Himself, Jesus said to them, "You know that those who are recognized as rulers of the Gentiles lord it over them; and their great men exercise authority over them. But it is not so among you, but whoever wishes to become great among you shall be your servant; and whoever wishes to be first among you shall be slave of all. For even the Son of Man did not come to be served, but to serve, and to give His life a ransom for many."

The room will get rather quiet as we see Jesus removing his robe, girding himself with a towel and washing the feet of even the one who will be responsible for having him on a cross in but a short while. Washing dirty feet? Being first means being last? Didn't come to be served but to serve? When the quietness fades, we begin to chatter like birds on a wire about what all that must mean and what it doesn't mean!

Why? Because it goes against our nature. If you are over me and I do what you tell me to do we will get along just fine because I will pose no threat to you. If I will recognize my place in comparison to you, all will go more smoothly in life. Except Jesus called this the Gentile way of doing life--and he doesn't want it in his kingdom. Then we suddenly remember a few verses that make us feel better about it all:

Servants, be submissive to your masters with all respect, not only to those who are good and gentle, but also to those who are unreasonable. I Pet 2:18

The above verse from Peter made us feel better because it is familiar. Masters and slaves. It resurrects up pictures of slaves sitting in their huts at night, singing, but not too loud lest the sound carries into the master's mansion...

But as the church is subject to Christ, so also the wives ought to be to their husbands in everything. Eph 5:24

Well, that one is OK, too. There are many men and women who feel comfortable with the unidirectional submission thing. We're carried back to the black and white days of television and we can almost hear June Cleaver, dressed in her pearls, asking Ward if he had a good day out killing beasts and carving out New York City! If that's the way you feel, you better not read the verse just before it, for it will send you on a full tilt. Some may never recover.

Every so often we think to give this concept of 'the last shall be first' a little try. Perhaps we brought it up in Sunday school or the preacher touched on it in the homily. Maybe it is that still small voice of reason as we search the Scriptures. Whatever it is, we are vowed to give it a try. And we do it that afternoon at the potluck.

I personally don't know where potlucks got started. Probably the same place that Sunday evening and Wednesday night got started. Wherever potlucks had their start, they are a very welcome idea to this preacher. It is a time to visit and get to know one another better (provided we don't bunch up into our regular bunches). It is a time to make visitors feel a little more welcome (provided we invite them) and newcomers will warm up rather quickly (provided we talk to them). But, of course, the best part is the food. Whatever one can say about Christian women, good or bad, we all must concede that they can cook--well! Indeed, as I recounted all that I would miss from full time preaching, those little extra big helpings and that slice of pie held back topped my list. But we decide, in the interest of the words of Christ, to do this potluck differently.

We're usually not the first in line. That is reserved for birthdays and special guests. But neither are we the last. Today, we will be the last. We busy ourselves with fetching napkins and drinks. We return to the kitchen to scoop ice and find a spatula for Sister Karen's casserole. En route, we might pluck a ripe olive off the salad tray, but olives are a biblical subject and certainly nothing wrong with that. Five more chairs are needed in the corner, another 5 gallons of punch and you are ready to get your plate.

And you find yourself in the end of the line, where you wanted to be. As you round the corner to pick up your paper plate and plastic ware, you recite the words of Jesus one more time to yourself: The last shall be first! Then you hit the table and notice that something went wrong, terribly wrong.

Ontology and Teleology [8]. Two words that need introducing at this point. Both, in a way, are concerned with cause and effect. Teleology is concerned with cause and effect leading to an endpoint here on earth. Ontology is concerned first with God as being the ultimate in cause and effect. Teleology is rooted here on earth with man's reason and experiences. Ontology is rooted in Heaven. A person who tries to experiment with Matthew 20:16 by waiting till all the food is gone and then expecting food is rooted in teleological thought. The person who waits till last, for the sheer joy of letting others enjoy a wide variety of food and cutting down on their wait in line time-- knowing that the food will run dangerously low and the majority of their time will be spent in line-- is rooted in ontological thought. That is submission and serving.

Oh, by the way, if you are standing next to a mountain or extremely large hill and praying real hard for the mountain to uproot itself and get tossed into the sea or a really large pond, and you're praying hard but you have one eye cracked open waiting for it all to happen because you read something in Mark 11:23 about this happening... then you are rooted in teleology, not ontology. Same lesson. Back to Christian submission and servitude.

When we submit and serve expressly for the pat on the back and the mention in the weekly bulletin or from the pulpit, we will be little better off than the Pharisee who, with arms flailing and trumpets blowing, prayed to God and gave to the poor on the street corner (Matt 6 is worth reading here). Serving is a gift, mentioned in Romans chapter 12, but it is also a mature act. It will not come from the spiritually immature.

Just take a moment to think about all that have placed submission one to another in their lives. There are some in your church family. Perhaps it is you. To be sure, some church families are messed up while some are riding the crest of greatness. Take out all that 'submit one to another' stuff and the bad will get worse and the crest riders will fizzle.

The Greek word *hupotasso* which is most often translated submit is in reality a military term. It simply means to line up under one's command. Anyone who has experienced combat (the place where this is ultimately tested) knows that if the command is strong by way of example, fearlessness, knowledge and a host of other virtues, the army will stick together and the battle will go well. If the command is weak, uncertain or fearful then watch out. You'll soon have a stampede on your hands of soldiers going the wrong direction.

Church, submit to your leaders (Heb 13:17) for they have an awesome responsibility. Leaders, are you worth submitting to? If not, they won't.

Wives, submit to your husbands as to the Lord (Eph 5:22). Husbands, are you worth submitting to? If not, they won't.

Children obey your parents in the Lord (Eph 6:1) for this is right. Parents, are you worth submitting to? If not, they won't.

Christians, submit one to another (Eph 5:21) in the fear of Christ. Church, are you mature enough to both give and get?

Peter summed up the idea of serving and submitting along with the reason to do so:

The end of all things is at hand; therefore, be of sound judgment and sober spirit for the purpose of prayer. Above all, keep fervent in your love for one another, because love covers a multitude of sins. Be hospitable to one another without complaint. As each one has received a special gift, employ it in serving one another, as good stewards of the manifold grace of God. Whoever speaks, let him speak, as it were, the utterances of God; whoever serves, let him do so as by the strength which God supplies; so that in all things God may be glorified through Jesus Christ, to whom belongs the glory and dominion forever and ever. Amen. I Pet 4:7ff

Agreeable doesn't necessitate that we buy any and everything that either comes down the pike or out of someone's mouth. No, that would be called gullible. We know all too well that there are some pretty crazy things that can drop down from someone's brain and into their mouth [9].

Being agreeable doesn't mean that we 'amen' it, just because we heard it--especially from the pulpit. But we all know what being disagreeable is. Note one brother in particular:

He was the **K**eeper **o**f the **B**ulletin **B**oards, or **KoBB** for short, and there were way plenty of the bulletin boards in this particular church building. Two-4x8 bulletin boards in the multipurpose room. Two of the same size in the foyer, plus four-3x6 bulletin boards. That church loved their messaging centers. Everything would go on the boards from church business, family accomplishments, gospel meetings for a 400 mile radius, pictures, newspaper clippings and even recipes. Brother KoBB would peruse the boards every Sunday morning, Sunday evening and midweek Bible study, with more attention paid to the boards than the Bible class. If he didn't like something, he simply took it down and threw it away!

Took a while to figure it all out. Kids were blamed. Preacher was blamed. Bulletin board gnomes were blamed, but it was KoBB. Brother KoBB was not hospitable because he wasn't agreeable. No one reading this would have agreed with everything on that board. No one's interests and beliefs run that wide. But we would have, hopefully, exercised a little hospitality in the matter. Now let's look at the second meaning of hospitable.

Being hospitable to one another without complaint was mentioned in Peter's words. The word *hospitable (philoxenos)* in the original Greek was a compound word that simply meant *lovers of strangers*. It took on a meaning, gathered from the contemporary writings of the time, that centered in and around the home. The idea behind the word was not hugging everyone you see at the mall, but exactly how we use it today: agreeable and treating guests with warmth and generosity. It meant to extend the same courtesy and blessings to those invited in as one would their own family. There's just something about a home.

Think about every time that you have been invited into someone's home, or you invited someone into your home. It may be someone you have worked with for months or longer. It may be someone you have worshipped with side by side for years. You know them, but yet you do not know them. You've shaken their hand. You've served with them on the

VBS committee. One summer you both took care of the church house lawn together.

But one evening in your house or theirs, laughing and stuffing your face, and you will never see them the same again. You will have built a bond that is not easily rattled by rumors or mistakes made. Split a pie and look over someone's gun collection, and the wrong answers in Bible class won't ruffle your feathers like they would otherwise. Swap stories about growing up and you will find yourself in that brother's defense next time instead of pecking them to death in the church house yard.

We think we know more than we really do about the first century church. How many times have you heard someone start a sentence with, "And in the first century church..." like it was all in one place, one culture, one language. Later on down the line the church was forced to meet in the tombs at night during the height of the Roman persecution. In the first century, however, as the church was forming here and there, they might have been free to meet in the synagogues (they were), the temple courts (they were), the riverside (they were) and a host of other places. What we do see is the church meeting in homes as early as the book of Acts. The phrase "and the church in their house," shows up in the letters of Romans, First Corinthians, Colossians and Philemon. Examine a map and look at the wide spread on those cities and note it was hardly a local custom. There's something about a house.

It's time to kick your doors open and invite some brethrens and sisterns in for some food, fun, and fellowship.

For you were called to freedom, brethren; only do not turn your freedom into an opportunity for the flesh, but through love serve one another. For the whole Law is fulfilled in one word, in the statement, "You shall love your neighbor as yourself." But if you bite and devour one another, take care lest you be consumed by one another. But I say, walk by the Spirit, and you will not carry out the desire of the flesh. Gal 5:13ff

We are members of one another and, therefore, mandated to be servants one to another showing submissiveness and hospitality. If mandated to live this way, we must pursue, not hinder these one another commands.

Questions for thought or discussion:

1. As a disciple of Christ, what does being a servant mean to you?

2. What does it mean to be submissive? What does it not mean? Show some specific examples.

3. As a disciple of Christ, does being submissive mean you always do what another disciple tells you to do? Explain or give examples.

4. List five behaviors you believe exemplify being hospitable.

5. What trait do you believe 'waiting for one another' when taking the Lord's supper represents (*cf* I Cor 11)? Justify your answer from Scripture.

Endnotes:

[8] Yes, yes, I know these words get a full run for the money in philosophical circles: extrinsic finality, utilitarian thought, eleatic monism, *etc., etc.,* but I'm keeping this in the monotheistic realm of Christianity (read: Bible)... What did he just say...?

[9] Or drop from brain onto keyboard. We call this e-mail. Plenty of mistakes made with this avenue of correspondence!

The Body: Not Passing Judgment, Lying, Speaking Evil, Challenging or Envying

We are members of one another and, therefore, mandated to not judge our brothers, especially through avenues of lying, talking down, provocation or envious attitudes that affect our behavior or speech. If mandated to live this way, we must pursue, not hinder these one another commands.

These are the negative commands. Not negative in a sense that they will bring about something bad or distasteful in our lives, but they rest in the Thou Shalt Not category. To be sure, if unheeded, they will bring about something bad or distasteful in our spiritual lives and among our spiritual brothers and sisters. Because they fall into the Thou Shalt Not category, they will take extra effort to effect in our lives. Loving one another, teaching one another and encouraging one another are all positive goals to attain. Sure, we have to get some things out of our lives in order to obtain those goals, but they remain positive nonetheless.

The Thou Shalt Not's have as a goal to stop and undo to the best of our ability. As adults, we don't like to be told what to do ("I get it, I get it! Just point me in the right direction and cut me loose!"). We especially do not like to be told to stop something. Perhaps it has to do with conjuring up a reenactment of our childhood when we grew oh so tired of being marched here and there and having our knuckles rapped. Perhaps it is tied into a seeming violation of a pecking order that we have dreamed up between our ears ("Don't tell me what to do!"). Whatever it is, we don't like it. We will stiffen our backs and lower our ears almost before the command to 'stop it!' completely hits our ears. But whether we like it or not, we have the allelon commands and they are listed here for convenience:

Therefore let us not judge one another anymore, but rather determine this-- not to put an obstacle or a stumbling block in a brother's way. Rom 14:13

Do not speak against one another, brethren. He who speaks against a brother, or judges his brother, speaks against the law, and judges the law; but if you judge the law, you are not a doer of the law, but a judge of it... Do not complain, brethren, against one another, that you yourselves may not be judged; behold, the Judge is standing right at the door. Jas 4:11 & 5:9

Do not lie to one another, since you laid aside the old self with its evil practices, Cols 3:9

But if you bite and devour one another, take care lest you be consumed by one another... Let us not become boastful, challenging one another, envying one another Gal 5:15 & 26

Therefore, laying aside falsehood, speak truth, each one of you, with his neighbor, for we are members of one another Eph 4:25

There they are. Not a complete list, just a list that contains our Greek word allelon in reference to one another. They don't seem as harsh when they are still passages out of the Bible that were written two millennia ago. It is when the passages are illustrated for us in our time and then application is made that they begin to deliver their sting. The Holy Spirit placed many more teachings like the above, just couched in other terms. Take for instance the idea of envying one another.

One Sunday morning in Bible class we began a study on envy. Two Sundays prior, we had held a class on jealousy where we explored, tore apart and picked through every aspect of jealousy that we could think of [10]. We gave examples from the Bible and from our own lives as well. We discussed keeping up with the Joneses and how we should react to our neighbor as he is out waxing his new bass tournament boat.

As the second bell rang, we decided (as always) that jealousy was a bad thing and that we should avoid it. Now, two weeks later, we're faced with the topic of envy. Class got off to a rockin' start, and it went something like...

"Well class, today is envy. It's a little like jealousy. What do y'all think envy is?"

"Well, it is probably like jealousy...yes, we think it is the same."

"Then, what do y'all think jealousy is?"

"Well. . .it's a little like being envious we think. Yes, to be jealous is to be envious."

And the faces beamed as we came up with an eternal vapor lock, defining one word by another and *vice versa*. But in English and koine Greek, the definitions couldn't be more different. Connected and sequential, but different. Let's take the time to separate these two terms.

Jealousy has two meanings. The first (and the way we don't use it in everyday conversation) has to do with fiercely guarding that which is yours (as in 'I am a jealous God'). The second meaning in both English and Greek of the day is that of seeking another's opportunity or possessions. This second meaning is the one we use everyday. It's the one we experience everyday. To be jealous is to be active. You are actively seeking someone's opportunity. You are actively seeking someone's possessions. Someone comes along and you are busted, exposed and humiliated. The excuses and justification come pouring forth like the Niagara. Envy is something else.

Envy precedes the actions that jealousy produce. It is internal. It is the discontent over another's advantage, situation or possessions. Nowhere in the Bible does envy shout louder than in the life of Jonah.

Jonah was given his assignment and it was a simple one: "Go tell the Ninevites that unless they change I will destroy them." Jonah departed but took a wrong turn at the boat docks. God caught up with him out in the middle of nowhere and asked him what was going on. Jonah clearly understood the request and assignment given to him by God, he just hadn't had time to internalize it and make it his own. God understood and allowed him three days of seclusion to think it over.

Understanding Body Life through the One Another Passages

If there was ever anything I wanted to see, it would be the last verse of Jonah chapter two. Maybe when we all get to Heaven there will be some way that we can see the movie. We also have no indication that there was a great lapse of time between Jonah 2:10 and the first verse of chapter 3. We see Jonah, standing there picking big fish stuff off his Old Testament robe while God asks him again to head into Nineveh and tell them that if they do not change that they will be destroyed. This time Jonah replied, "Let's go!"

Jonah blows into the city crying, "Turn or burn, heed or Hell." He doesn't even get a third of the way through his sermon before folks are not only heading down to the front pew to fill out a response card, they're bringing their donkeys along, filling out response cards for them as well! It should have been the greatest day in Jonah's life.

I have preached and taught for many years. I begged and pleaded and reasoned from the Scriptures. I saw the looks on people's faces that said, "One more minute and you would have had me." I showed them Heaven, and I showed them Hell, yet at the invitation the most I ever saw respond publicly was, perhaps, six at any one time. Jonah had 120,000. Imagine, deacons on roller blades delivering boxes of response cards while the church sings all six verses of *Just As I Am* one hundred and fifty three times!

But Jonah was sore. He was pouting. He was sulking. He was envious, discontented over another's advantage or situation. He told God, "Look, I knew you were going to do this anyway. What do you need me for? I could be dead and it wouldn't matter anyway." He was discontented at the good in someone else's life.

That's a dumb way to be. Imagine, being all bent out of shape because something good happened to someone else. The same was true of the Elder Brother in Luke chapter 15.

The Prodigal Son had returned. He was skinny, stinky and stunned. The Father, however, was ecstatic, exuberant and elated. The Festival Calf was nervous. The music and dancing mushroomed as the party began and folks began pouring through the door. Upon returning from another 'backbreaking day in the field,' the Elder Brother heard the celebration and exclaimed, "What's that noise?" He wasn't really asking a question in order to seek an answer. He was making a statement of dissatisfaction. He was angry and discontented at the good in someone else's life. His own brother's life.

That's a dumb way to be. Imagine, being all bent out of shape because something good happened to someone else.

Envy caused the Elder Brother to stand outside in the cold night air, watching the party inside. Envy led to pride as he shrugged off the Father's hand as it invited him inside for the celebration. Envy caused Jonah to lay sunburned under a dead vine while a dry wind stifled his mumbling so that no one but God could hear. His mumbling of discontent was matched by a worm munching on the vine.

That's a dumb way to be. Imagine, being all bent out of shape because something good happened to someone else.

Yet Paul, through the Galatian churches, tells us today not to be that way. In the same verse (5:26) he warns them neither to envy one another or challenge one another. Keep in mind that the word church is 'those who are called out.' Compare **church** to the word **challenge** which is 'those who are called before.' It is literally calling someone before you for a fight. That's a dumb way for a church to be, yet it's possible because we have warnings not to. But we know all too well from our own experience that envy is possible. So are the other Thou Shalt Not's from our master list. Lying, for instance, is something that we have perfected into an art form over the course of our lives.

Just as we defined envy, so we should spend a little time on lying. Ask anyone what lying is all about. They will give you one of two answers: 1- they will say that they don't know what lying means (which, you will note, is a lie) or, 2- they will say that lying is saying, or telling, something that isn't true. I don't believe that--and you don't either. It's too simplistic and misses the point.

Go back and look at that second definition again. Simply saying something that isn't true. I don't believe that--and you don't either. Again, it is too simplistic and missed the point.

We say things all the time that aren't true, yet they aren't a lie in and of themselves. For instance, you return home from work and notice that Aunt Mabel's car isn't in the driveway. You come in and while you are hanging your coat up the phone rings. It's for Aunt Mabel (it's Myrtle with the bridge club), and you tell them she isn't there and you really don't know what time to expect her back but you would be ever so happy to take a message. You write down Myrtle's phone number and go on about your evening's rat killing. About thirty minutes later, Aunt Mabel comes down the stairs with pronounced nap hair. She startles you as you ask her where she's been. The story unfolds that her car is in the shop, Velma drove her home, and she has been taking a nap. You give her the Myrtle message and go on.

Did you tell Myrtle something that wasn't true? You bet. There wasn't an ounce of truth in your reply. She was home and you weren't expecting her because she was only thirty feet away from you. However, with as much untruth as all of that contained, you don't feel compelled to rush to the phone to call the president of the bridge club and beg for forgiveness. You really don't expect the whole neighborhood to show up at your door chanting, "Li-ar! Li-ar! Pants on Fi-ar!" You have absolutely no plans whatsoever to crawl down front on the next Sunday's altar call, covered in ashes, while the entire church sings *Just As I Am*.

Now let's take this from a 'whoops, shucks' example into something more mature and more intense. Your good friend of over forty years is in the hospital. She has been battling cancer for several years now and it looks as if she won't be leaving this time other than via the funeral home. You saw her two days ago and the day before that, but you want to spend as much time with her as you can. Keys in hand, you cut short your evening's plans and head out the door.

As you pass the nurse's station, you inquire on her condition. They reply, "She's awake," which, you know, isn't an answer to your question but at the same time answers your question. As the door opens, you can smell the one smell that we all deeply dislike. We dislike it because it reminds all of us of the great equalizer--death. Your friend looks horrible. You've never seen her this bad before. You can only imagine the physical and emotional pain she must be feeling. Her face is sullen and her skin an ashen green. Her eyes don't have that sparkle that you remember for all those decades. Her hair is a total mess, all the body and shine chemically knocked out from the treatments--what little there is left of the hair. The conversation between you goes something like this:

"Louise? Are you awake?"

"Oh, Margie. Oh, I wish I knew you were coming so I could get ready."

"You needn't bother. Well, I thought about calling, but didn't want to wake you if you were sleeping. If you were asleep now, I would have just come back. Wanted to see how you were doing."

"Well, I'm a mess. I look a mess (as she flips the mirror up on the table top, trying not to burst out in tears). I look terrible without any makeup. Look at these eyes!" Her hands begin to shake more, and tears are now coming freely to her eyes. The ball is now in your court.

"No, you look fine, Louise. I believe you look better than you did earlier this week. You must be feeling better."

"I look horrible. I don't even look like me. Look at my eyes and my hair."

"You look the same as the young girl I sat next to in chemistry class. You haven't changed one little bit..." And the conversation goes on. Any untruths in the conversation? You betcha. Count them out! Margie tossed 'em out one after another after another. I'm afraid that if some of my brethren were to have their shot at Louise they would have told her that she smelled bad, looked bad and looked like she was going to die! Some of my brethren have camels wedged in their throats and gnats in their teeth, too.

So what is a lie? To be sure, it's an untruth. But it is also something that is deliberately told (or left unsaid?--nope, we'll get to that one later) to cause the conclusion of the listener to be swayed in such a way as to give an advantage to the speaker. It is something that is said in order to hide an object or hide from a consequence. It is something that is said in order to 'one up' the listener. It is something that is said to make the listener believe that the speaker is something that he isn't. It is something that is said in order to dislodge some object, or opportunity, or cash out of the hands of the listener into the hands of the speaker. It is a wall, a mask, and it is not OK.

I'm told by antologists that ants cover great distances (relative to an ant) by simply rubbing their antennas with the oncoming ant to see where he's been. This is how they keep their trails consistent across your backyard or kitchen floor. Suppose there is a malicious ant in the bunch--one that found a Twinkie under the davenport--that wants to throw off everyone else so that he can come back later and have the creamy center to himself? The first ant he comes to will ask him (through rubbing), "Did you find anything?" to which malicious ant will rub back, "No, especially not any Twinkies with any creamy centers. But if you will move the trail a little to your left..."

Chaos. Ants everywhere. Now think of the church. We see by the allelon commands that we are all part of one another. We rely on each other to get the work and will of the Father carried out. We are hands, eyes, feet, knuckles and knees. Throw in one lie, one liar, and soon there are Christians scurrying everywhere and no Twinkies are being hauled in. Satan loves it when he can disrupt the Twinkie harvest.

This might be a good place to throw in a short discussion on the word *guile* or *deceit*. From the Greek word *dolos*, it is only found eleven times in the New Testament. Of all the times it is used, Peter used it foundationally to state that Jesus had no guile (*cf* Pet 2:22). Different from lying? Just a little. Think of it more like a hybrid lie, since it is actually the word for bait. Yep, bait, like going fishing.

Think about it. How many times have you heard or said, "No, no, no! I NEVER told him that! He decided that stuff on his own!" Did he really, or did he take the bait you threw out intentionally in his way? Guile is a tactic to attempt to skate out from under responsibility. Do we need to go farther? I think not, but remember that although there is no specific [11] command against baiting one another, it is simply a hybrid form of lying. It's time to clean up our lives.

Lying and gossip seem to go hand in hand. Where one is, the other is not usually far behind. Gossip may, or may not, contain lies, though its expected endpoint is usually the same. It is intended to bait and tear down. It is intended to judge. It is truly the church's weapon of mass destruction. In Romans chapter 14, Paul tells us not to judge one another. James calls it speaking against one another in chapter 4 and then equates it with judging both our brother and the law of Christ. In that same verse (v. 11), James shows us the impossibility of both judging the law and being a doer of the law. Those who judge and speak against a brother cannot be a participator of that law. If we don't participate in the law of Christ...

Speaking against is a descriptive word in the original language. At times, our English language seems to be bankrupt when placed next to koine Greek. We rely on adjectives and adverbs, for the most part, to get our ideas emphasized. The Greeks had emphatic words. One such word is *katalaleo*, a compound word simply meaning to *speak down*.

Think about it. That's what lying and gossip are: speaking down to a brother or sister. You strip away their dignity when you lie, withholding the truth. You strip away any chance of dignity (human nature being what it is) when you gossip about them. You place them in the gutter as if they were so much trash waiting for the street sweeper. Consider the practical application test for gossip:

1. Is it true? Get all the facts. Your perception of the person must be checked out and be true.

2. Is it fair to all concerned? Is it right?

3. Is it speech that will bring good will and promote God's cause?

4. Is it full of the character of God?

5. Is it your business?

As I have presented the Five Steps of Gossip over the years, many have commented that number five should really be number one. True. Sometimes things are listed last for emphasis. If it ain't your business, it ain't your business. Therefore, stay out of it, because trying to undo gossip, lying and slander is next to impossible.

When I was little, I heard the story of the lad who told some lies and got folks into trouble, in an uproar, and all the other disruptions that come with lying. Feeling bad, the lad went to the Wise Old Preacher and asked what he could do to take back all the lies. The Wise Old Preacher gave him a box of feathers and told him to place a feather on the stoop of everyone he lied to or about, then return. Upon return, the Wise Old Preacher told him to now go reclaim all those feathers. The lad, sadly, found that all the feathers had been scattered by the afternoon breeze. His box remained empty. Then, in the wisdom that only a Wise Old Preacher could give to a young lad, the Wise Old Preacher relayed, "You see, my child, lies are like a feather. Once you put them out you can never gather them in again." The lad gave the empty box back to the Wise Old Preacher, hung his head low and went home.

Sounds good, except that just about every place I've lived, the wind blows constantly. One would never get the feather out of the box, let alone place it on a set of stairs. It would only work in Syracuse, NY. Besides, why in the world would a preacher have a box of feathers laying around in his office anyway? Is that the difference between a regular preacher and a Wise Old Preacher? Gimme a break! I prefer the Pizza Party illustration.

You know the place. Puppets of rats and birds and bears all singing the same old songs every 15 minutes while kids run amuck waiting on the overpriced pizza. You give the 453 children you invited each a hundred tokens, knowing that will only keep them occupied for 14 minutes tops. You keep one token for yourself and you wander over to the skee ball--and promptly do lousy at it. It is then you notice that a kid running through drops a token. Disappearing into a sea of children, you know you will never find that kid again, so you do the next best thing--try a game of Bop the Weasel!

You've tried it. Don't lie [12]. It's the one where you put your token in and pick up this giant rubber mallet and stare at the holes in the game board. In a split second the weasel pops his head up. You are too slow! He ducks and runs before your mallet can contact the board. You must work faster. Then, the hole to the lower left produces a weasel. The same weasel with the same grin on its face. Again, too slow. Your mallet does little damage. Again, top right. Again, middle hole. The weasels are coming faster and faster. Some you bop. Most you don't. One thing's for sure and don't miss the lesson: even if you bop it once, twice, multiple times, it keeps coming back!

Once you tell the lie, once you talk down a brother, once you tear down a sister, once you challenge a fellow disciple, you can bop it with all the 'I'm Sorry's' and all the repentance in the world and it will keep coming back. You can slither down the aisle on Sunday morning while the entire church sings *Just As I Am*, all the while hitting yourself in the face with a songbook, and the lie and slander will keep coming back at you for a long time. The same one that disrupts the Twinkie harvest is the one that keeps throwin' the weasel back into play. It is easier, far easier, to never unleash the weasel in the first place.

One last thought on this section, and that is about judgment. The cry to judge or not judge is, at times, misused. How many times in a Bible class has someone brought up a wrong act or a false belief that someone holds, only to be met with, "You're judging them. You shouldn't judge someone. The Bible says not to judge someone!"? In fact, every time anyone brings up something that a group or an individual or an outfit is saying, believing or doing wrong it is met by that not-so-still small voice in the back of the class declaring, "We shouldn't judge. Bible says not to judge! Matthew 7:1 states plainly, 'Judge not, that ye be not judged.'" After a while, the conversation and discussion drops to nil on the fear of being told once again to 'judge not.'

It is true. Jesus said very plainly that we shouldn't judge, because we would be judged also. So what gives? The allelon commands clearly contain a 'let us not judge one another' as does the aforementioned command of Jesus from the Sermon on the Mount. What are we to do, especially in the light of the following command:

Do not judge according to appearance, but judge with righteous judgment. Jno 7:24

It's not a trick. Same Greek word (*krino*) with the same

Greek meaning (judge, decide) used in Matthew 7:1 and John 7:24. Either we are, or we aren't. What gives? Is the not-so-still small voice in the back of the class correct? Are we to just let everyone do as they please and let them be their own decision maker? Should we never say anything to anyone, especially a brother or sister, because we run the risk of judging?

Hardly. It all might sound great in a very postmodern society, but it isn't Bible.

Let's begin by examining the person with the not so-still small voice in the back of the room. Every church family has one, or two or fifteen. As we examine this individual, let us not forget the allelon lessons thus far. To begin with, we are after peace and harmony in the body of Christ. Second, we must forbear with one another with kindness. We have the mandate to teach and admonish one another, but we also have the mandate to encourage, not tear down.

To begin with, this person may have been beat up in the church, or someone close to this person was beat up by the brethren. Not physically, but verbally. Emotionally. Psychologically. Perhaps they 'judged' someone and incurred the wrath of the many. They don't want it to happen again, or don't want it to happen to someone else- especially within their line of sight.

Perhaps this person, more than likely, has a loved one who has departed from the faith and is no longer in a standing relationship with the Lord. It grieves this person on a continual basis and any reminder from folks hashing and rehashing anyone who has left the Lord only deepens the feelings. They cry, "Don't judge!" as a survival mechanism so the pain will not grow any more intense.

As a last possibility, they may have witnessed the breakup of a family. Not the breakup of a physical family, as common as the phenomena is in this day, age and society, but the breakup of a spiritual one. They've seen brethren stand up in the middle of Sunday services and announce loudly that, "God has judged this church and finds it to be lacking, therefore, we must remove ourselves and worship elsewhere with the true saints of our Lord," or some such grandiose nonsense. Perhaps (and maybe because of the blinders caused by one of the above scenarios) the person either has not fully understood what Jesus was beginning to say in Matthew 7:1, finished in verse two and illustrated in verses three through five. Look closely at it again.

In verses one and two, Jesus said that however we choose to judge, that standard will be used on us. If we judge by the petty and certainly self serving ways that the world would judge folks then that standard will be used on us. If we are using the true standard of judgment, which is the Word of God, then we will be judged by that same standard. If we use it correctly, inclusive of mercy and grace, then mercy and grace will be shown us. If we use it harshly, then as quickly and as harshly as we deal it out, it will be dealt back to us in like manner.

As disciples of Christ, since we use the Word of God to judge mankind (which is the correct standard to use!), there are just certain lifestyles and actions that God has already spoken about. This is what Jesus meant in John 7:24.

He doesn't want us to judge by appearance, whether that be a person's physical appearance or by a cursory examination of what we think is happening, or going on inside someone's head (motives). He wants us to use a righteous judgment, which is always and always will be the Word of God. Already written down. Never changing. Always applicable in all time zones, cultures and races.

Therefore, teaching a brother, because we see something amiss in his life or something falling far short of what God would want, is not judgment. Admonishing the unruly for the same reason is not judgment. Biting and devouring one another, speaking down to, or about, a brother is worldly judgment. Complaining about and lying to a brother is worldly judgment.

Rest assured that worldly judgment will come back on us exactly how we measure it out to each other. This is Jesus' promise to those who do so, put down in pen and ink in Matthew 7:2. When we use the Word of God as a standard within the family of God (operating the church by design), the family of God will be blessed beyond all we can ask or think. This is Jesus' promise in Matthew 7:2.

We are members of one another and, therefore, mandated to not judge our brothers, especially through avenues of lying, talking down, provocation or envious

Understanding Body Life through the One Another Passages

attitudes that affect our behavior or speech. If mandated to live this way, we must pursue, not hinder these one another commands.

Questions for thought or discussion:

1. Develop a list of 'tests' a disciple could use to prevent passing judgment on another disciple. Is this list necessarily tied to a church building setting?

2. Explain why you think disciples are tempted to not tell the truth?

3. Give three examples of how one disciple can speak evil of another.

4. Explain three ways one disciple can provoke another disciple.

5. List five guidelines a disciple can use to avoid provoking another disciple.

6. How can you avoid envying? What are the specific steps you will take?

Endnotes:

[10] Before this was a book, it was a 13 week series of Sunday School lessons. With the questions at the ends of each section, it still can be.

[11] of the allelon type

[12] especially since we're in the section about not lying to one another!!

The Body: Welcoming and Loving

We are members of one another and, therefore, are mandated to welcome and love one another. If mandated to live this way, we must pursue, not hinder these one another commands.

This section is not long, however, this section will take a lifetime to complete for it will never be completed in one's lifetime. It has no endpoint.

"We want to say, 'Welcome!' to all of our regular folks and especially extend a great big church 'Welcome!' to all of our visitors. We're especially thankful that you could join us this morning in songs and praise to our Lord. We hope that you will return each and every Lord's day that you are able to do so. In the meantime, please locate and fill out a visitor's card that you will find in the back of the pew in front of you. Later, during the collection, please feel free to drop it in the plate or simply leave it in the pew to be picked up later. You will find us an especially friendly bunch here at the First Faith & Grace Apostolic Holiness Church of the Redeemed. To prove that, I'm going to ask everyone to stand as you meet and greet each other and especially our visitors. We want to make you feel ever so special."

That particular announcement, or something close to it, can be heard in church buildings on any given Sunday morning all across the country. It's not even unique to the USA, for one Sunday morning in Mexico City, the first words I heard were, "Buenas dias y bienvenidos a los servicios de Ia Iglesia Centro..."

And there is nothing wrong with it. In our culture, there are a couple of things right about it. It helps break the ice when a stranger comes into our midst. It gives two people, who haven't said heidi-ho to each other all week, a chance to do so. However, it fades in comparison to the first century idea of welcoming or greeting one another. Let's look at that first century middle eastern concept of greeting one another in the light of a directive Jesus gave his seventy disciples as he sent them out on the limited commission:

Now after this the Lord appointed seventy others, and sent them two and two ahead of Him to every city and place where He Himself was going to come. And He was saying to them, *"The harvest is plentiful, but the laborers are few; therefore beseech the Lord of the harvest to send out laborers into His harvest. Go your ways; behold, I send you out as lambs in the midst of wolves. Carry no purse, no bag, no shoes; and* **greet no one on the way***. And whatever house you enter, first say, 'Peace be to this house.' And if a man of peace is there, your peace will rest upon him; but if not, it will return to you.* Luke 10:1-6

Seems strange to us today. Not the part about grown men carrying purses, but the command from Christ to greet no one along the way. Sounds rather standoffish and highfalutin to us today. Why would someone want seventy men out preaching to walk around in robes with purses and their nose out of joint? Even in the part of the country I'm from, it is customary while driving to at least give someone the 'hi sign' as you pass them. Answer--we haven't considered what went into the first century middle eastern idea of greeting. In short, we failed to understand a Bible passage in its context! [13]

It could be, and often was, elaborate. Traveling on foot was the only mode of travel in those times, with the exception of the occasional donkey--which isn't much faster. Because of economics and a safety factor, large families or groups of people would often band together to travel from one town to another. The story recorded in Luke chapter two of Jesus lagging behind in Jerusalem while his family took off back to Galilee is one glimpse we have in Scripture of this mode of travel. They were three days out of Jerusalem before they even knew he was missing, supposing him to be somewhere in the caravan within the safety of some relatives.

Imagine what it would be like for one large group to meet another large group head on along the way. Take a moment and create the visual picture. Being a custom of the times, they would all stop, dismount any animals they may be riding, and see if anyone was related to anyone. It was the postal route and family reunion all rolled into one. If they found they were kinfolk, everyone would have to hug everyone, kiss everyone and then make plans to spend a great portion of the afternoon with each other. Maybe pitch a tent and chase down a fatted calf or two. It would be a little like Jacob & fam meeting Esau & fam in Genesis chapter 33. In our rush-around-world in cars doing 70 mph and cell phones, we are pretty near worn out by the time Jacob and Esau depart, what with all that bowing down and introductions! When folks then would travel to and from Jerusalem or other trips of business, they would wind up having a family vacation at the same time.

When Jesus sent out his twelve and then his seventy, he sent them on a limited commission both geographically and time wise. He didn't want all of their time and effort tied up on the side of the road visiting with long lost relatives and picking their teeth after snacking on fatted calves. They had a job to do and he wanted them to get on it. In its context of time and culture, Jesus' words make sense to us. Imagine us carrying out the limited commission today and not succumbing to all the distractions that we become snagged with: eating, sightseeing, eating, visiting among ourselves, eating, television, eating--and the list goes on.

Aspadzomai is the Greek word that is translated *greet* in the New Testament. It isn't a heidi-ho word but rather a word of action from the heart. It is full of emotion and wishes for a desired effect. It is the word used when Mary traveled far to visit her relative Elizabeth. Upon entering her house, Mary greeted her. I believe that we can all discount Mary simply giving Elizabeth a quick hug, a heidi-ho and a cursory inquiry (after a slap on the back) into how she was getting along.

Aspadzomai is the word chosen in Mark chapter nine when Jesus descended from the mount of transfiguration, only to find his remaining disciples in a full blown discussion with a crowd of people including some Scribes. When they all saw Jesus, they rushed to greet him. No heidi-ho there, but a serious matter of a little boy caught in the grips of a demon. It is also the word Mark chose in chapter 15 verse 18 when he said that the soldiers, after putting a robe on Jesus and crunching a crown of thorns on his head, were *acclaiming* him 'King of the Jews.' Verse 19 illustrates for us the effort that they were putting into it.

Aspadzomai is the word Luke used in Acts to show us King Agrippa and Bernice paying their respect to Festus. Unlikely is it that Agrippa simply backslapped Festus and gave him a heidi-ho along with comments about the weather and a first century equivalent quip about a pro-football team. We may have all kinds of terms for what Agrippa did to Festus, but one thing is for sure: Festus was buttering the bread and Agrippa knew it.

Aspadzomai is the word used over and over in Romans chapter 16. Heidi-ho just doesn't fit into Romans chapter 16. It just doesn't.

In Hebrews chapter 11 we are told several things about faith. We're told that it is impossible to please God without it. We're told that the ancients of old lived by it. We're told that their faith let them glimpse Heaven while on earth:

All these died in faith, without receiving the promises, but having seen them and having welcomed (aspazomai) them from a distance, and having confessed that they were strangers and exiles on the earth. Heb 11:13

By now, we should be convinced that Biblical greeting goes far beyond shaking hands in a church house foyer or stumbling over pews for sixty seconds to shake a total stranger's hand. It is active, proactive. It gets into someone else's life. It lifts masks and inspects the underside. It plows under layers and reveals. It accomplishes tasks and doesn't simply take notes. Biblical greeting fills and warms.

I'm not down on heidi-hos, foyer greeters or a time of 'meet n' greet' during the worship service (OK, maybe a little bit). I am down on this being considered an endpoint, somehow fulfilling a Biblical doctrine or two. When we are mandated to greet one another, we are called to something much deeper than the handshake and the pat on the back.

Churches worry, and always have and will, about numerical growth. The one I was preaching for at the time was no exception. Across town was a group that was seeming to grow by leaps and bounds and my elders wanted to know why, for it was feared they would suck the life out of our family if left unchecked. It was decided that one Sunday my family and I would attend their worship and take notes, much as the spies did who pulled off that Jericho thing. The Sunday came and the four of us pulled into the parking lot. My mental note pad was in full swing.

We entered the church building. A designated man was standing by the doorway into the sanctuary with programs in hand. He handed me one, being the alpha male of the little pack, and mumbled a heidi-ho as we passed. There were several hundred already ahead of us, all sitting down and facing forward as if waiting for the raising of the curtain at the local theater. We located a pew midway and, hoping that we weren't squatting, filed in and sat down to total silence. To be sure, some were visiting amongst themselves, but to my family of four it was total silence. One family came by, paused, and smiled. They went on a few rows and then doubled back behind us. The message was clear: we had taken their pew!

The service started on time and followed the program flawlessly. There were announcements followed by a prayer and some songs. The choir sang and the pastor spoke about Ephesians chapter 4. He said the Greek said something that it didn't say. A little like someone telling you the Spanish word *mensa* means *bright* and *intelligent*. There was another song followed by a prayer of dismissal. I was still choking on the Greek stuff. When all rose to exit, one elderly lady behind us remarked, "My, you two sing well."

I took it as a compliment. I would have much rather had some interaction. I would have been happy to give her my name, my wife's name and the name of my two boys. I would have listened carefully for her name and her friend's name. I would not have even minded a little conversation about the weather and the local pro football team.

And that was it. That was the sum total of our interaction with hundreds of folks as we slowly made our way out of the church building. My imaginary note pad folded and ink pen capped with a mental note of no entry. We reentered our vehicle and drove off the lot. My report on 'church growth' was simply this: don't waste your time looking for it in their auditorium on Sunday morning. It isn't there. It might be in a Mother's Day Out program but it isn't in the hour dedicated to the vertical by the horizontal worshipers. As we passed that particular church building over the next several months, my two boys then aged five and nine begged us never to go back there again. Out of the mouth of babes... The vertical crumbled long ago when the horizontal played out.

That's what greeting isn't. What is it? Nowhere in my life has it ever been brought closer to what God had in mind than in Turkey, Texas in the 1980's. I certainly hope some of them are reading this and smiling--for I know that God did.

Laugh if you want. I certainly did. I was a drilling supervisor for Gulf Oil at the time and when they told me I'd be drilling a wildcat in Turkey, I immediately ran the checklist through my mind of passports and inoculation shots, wondering if I liked that kind of coffee. I then found out it would be Turkey, Texas with a population of 600 on a good day. I checked into the Turkey Hotel waiting for my drilling equipment and crews to arrive. I drove through town (a thirty second task) and found the church building I wanted to attend. I instinctively knew that the church building would contain the church.

Equipment arrived and we started drilling five miles south of town. Sunday rolled around and I was able to dart off at the last minute to join the brethren. Already missing Bible class (which I personally feel is the first half of Sunday morning worship--how 'bout you?) I arrived a few minutes before the second half began. Being conscious of what I might be tracking in, I had thrown on a pair of clean company coveralls and decided to ditch my boots at the door and go in with stocking feet. Anyone who has worked with the yuck and frump of oil well drilling knows from whence I speak. I could hardly get my boots off for having to shake hands and visit. Finding a pew about three quarters of the way back, I sat down. Soon another man came up to me.

He asked if I was a brother in Christ. I assured him, yes. He asked if I would be interested in assisting with the Lord's supper, or communion. Instinctively my mind raced to my stocking feet and my mouth voiced my concerns. His reply? "Brother, that isle ain't a runway for a girl's fashion show. It's an aisle to walk up and down to pass out communion." Soon, myself and three others were standing in front of the family of God as one brother led our minds in prayer before the supper was passed.

As with everyone, there was a closing prayer. Folks once again began to engage me in visitation. Many asked me to stay for the monthly potluck to follow. So far, so normal: Sunday morning worship followed by potluck. Invitation to stay. Invitation declined because I had to return to work.

I drove off back to the rig hoping to find every thing decent and in order. I did, and settled down to an afternoon of switching between watching the rotary table go around and around, and watching one of the two television stations that I was able to pick up (satellite TV? Um, NO!). Being what is termed in the oilfield as a 'closed hole,' meaning that information is not given out and the site is off limits to folks driving up, I pretty soon was adrift into an unconscious state on that Sunday afternoon. I was awakened by one of the rig hands entering my trailer house with the warning that, "A Chevy Suburban just drove in and it looks like a bunch of folks from town."

It was. It was my brothers and sisters from the church. I'm not able to make the potluck? Then the potluck came to me: Fresh quail and homemade ice cream. I'm just sure there was a green bean casserole in there somewhere. Not all could, but some stayed and visited for hours. We talked about the drilling (in general!). We talked about the church in Turkey. We talked about the family where I was from. We read some from the Bible and talked about what we read.

With over a year's worth of drilling in and around that area, working nine days on and five days off, I felt that this was my home away from home. I was included. I was built up. I was part of the family. I was biblically greeted and biblically welcomed. I was the recipient of what Paul had in mind when he closed his letter to the Philippians:

And my God shall supply all your needs according to His riches in glory in Christ Jesus. Now to our God and Father be the glory forever and ever. Amen. Greet every saint in Christ Jesus. The brethren who are with me greet you. All the saints greet you, especially those of

Caesar's household. The grace of the Lord Jesus Christ be with your spirit.

Greeting is an allelon, or one another, command. It carries us much, much farther than the handshake and the heidi-ho of the church house foyer. We have only fooled ourselves if we begin and end with the little room that separates the front door from the sanctuary as we move to and fro from our cars to our pews.

If we can't greet one another, if we can't greet those of the household of faith, if we can't greet those outside of the faith looking in, then we will not be able to love one another. We can't. We won't have either the foundational basis or the tools.

As the title of this section suggests, we are to love one another. All my life I have heard sermons and Sunday schools on the subject of loving one another. All through ministry training I heard classes taught on the subject of love. I have delivered many sermons and classes myself on the subject of loving one another, knowing the full ramifications of attempting to bypass this awesome command. Let's take a few minutes to look through the Scriptures again on the subject of love.

A new commandment I give to you, that you love one another, even as I have loved you, that you also love one another. By this all men will know that you are My disciples, if you have love for one another. Jno 13:34f

Owe nothing to anyone except to love one another; for he who loves his neighbor has fulfilled the law. Rom 13:8

For you were called to freedom, brethren; only do not turn your freedom into an opportunity; for the flesh, but through love serve one another. For the whole Law is fulfilled in one word, in the statement, You shall love your neighbor as yourself But if you bite and devour one another, take care lest you be consumed by one another. Gal 5:13-15

Now may our God and Father Himself and Jesus our Lord direct our way to you; and may the Lord cause you to increase and abound

in love for one another, and for all men, just as we also do for you;
I Thess 3:11f

Since you have in obedience to the truth purified your souls for a sincere love of the brethren, fervently love one another from the heart, for you have been born again not of seed which is perishable but imperishable, that is, through the living and abiding word of God.
I Pet 1:22f

Above all, keep fervent in your love for one another, because love covers a multitude of sins. I Pet 4:8

They all looked familiar, didn't they. The reason is that we have been discussing them all along while we have looked at ministry gifts, the relationship between the vertical and horizontal, forbearance, welcoming and forgiving one another and not tearing one another down. Love is a big category. It is Body Life.

Love cannot be studied in one Sunday school class. It cannot be finished in one chapter of a Bible study guide or covered in one sermon. It is more than Roman numeral one in an outline--it is the outline. It is more than the first item on the agenda--it is the agenda. We do it a disservice by attempting to break it down into a smaller part. It is not Lesson 6 of a 13 week course of study.

In Matthew chapter 22, Jesus was once again posed a question in an attempt to trip him up. What the leading Jews didn't know was that in their little quest to stump the preacher they were gathering for us the greatest example of the vertical intersecting the horizontal that we could ever hope to have.

The Jews wanted to know what the greatest commandment was. No, technically they knew what it was. They wanted to know if Jesus was on the same time honored tradition page that they were on. He was, and much more. To love God was the greatest commandment that anyone could follow. I really don't know what answer they expected Jesus to give them. Maybe they expected something different than what he gave them or they wouldn't have asked. He gave them the correct answer, then took the opportunity to shed more insight into it. Isn't that a neat tactic? -- "Oh, and since you asked ..." Jesus truly is the Master Teacher!

Since the horizontal relationship with God is defined by our actions here on earth, to leave the answer as simply to love the Lord your God with all your heart, and with all your soul, and with all your mind is to show the incomplete. Clean up your room and take out the trash. Without both, the chores are not done. Repent and be baptized. One without the other does little good. Love God and love your neighbor as yourself. Don't love neighbor? Don't claim to love God. Don't bother him with your life's offerings. That is the message of Matthew 5:24. That is the message of Malachi.

I remember well a man I visited with, or tried to, about his absence from Body Life. Most would just say that he 'quit coming to church.' Reports were that he got upset, mad, nose out of joint over something that the church was doing, wanted to do, talked about (you pick) and he grabbed his marbles and took off. Months and a few years passed and I asked him about his situation. He replied that he was just fine with God, he and God had an understanding but those no good bunch of hypocritters down at the church building were not worth two cents and he didn't want to hang out with a bunch of no good, rotten... You've seen the movie. With the path of the horizontal long overgrown with thistles and briars, the vertical was just a vapor trail. Love for one another is a must in our relationship with God. It is all encompassing in our dealing with one another.

In Colossians chapter three, Paul is directing us to rid ourselves of certain behaviors and traits (fornication, idolatry, wrath) and replace them with certain desired qualities (kindness, compassion, forgiveness). When the list is finished, he states in verse 14:

And beyond all these things put on love, which is the pefect bond of unity.

Why? Because love is the big picture. It is the glue in the pressboard. It is the egg and cheese in the casserole. It is the rubber band around the stack of bills. It is the belt around your waist. It holds everything together. It is the same point that Paul was making in First Corinthians chapter 13 when he showed the church that faith, hope and love would long outlive the scrambling around and bickering over the miraculous gifts of tongues and divine prophecies, which were destined for the woodpile. Faith, hope and love would all be around, but the binder would be love.

It is one thing to recognize love as a binder and another to define it. If we don't have a working model of what love is, then we will either fail to exercise it or we will miss the train and be carrying it out in a misguided way. Scripture will teach us through the three major ways that the Bible teaches: Didactic, example or comparison. Didactic is a fancy term for teaching. Think college lecture. This is the Ten Commandments. This is God telling Moses exactly how to build the tabernacle. This is Paul's list of do and don't that we briefly mentioned in Colossians chapter three. This is Paul's style throughout most of First Corinthians.

Comparison is common throughout the New Testament, where we have centered our thoughts on. "The Kingdom of Heaven is like...," is one such comparison found throughout Matthew chapter 13. Indeed, all the parables are a type of comparison, drawing similarities between everyday items and occurrences and spiritual teachings. Paul's comparison of the Law of Moses and the new covenant in Galatians, and Jude's comparisons of his day's false teachers and those of antiquity are still other types of comparison teaching.

Example is our third large type of teaching in the Scriptures. Jesus said often, "Go and do likewise." Paul told the Corinthian church twice in his first letter, "Be imitators of me," and wanted the church in Thessalonica to remember his behavior and speech while he was with them and duplicate it. Peter's appeal to fellow shepherds in First Peter chapter 5 would fall into this category. The first teaching on love will be from the example category.

The stories can be read in Matthew chapter 19, Luke chapter 18 or Mark chapter 10. The various writers recorded different questions that had been posed to Jesus. Some were designed to heckle him. Some were serious, or so it seems, queries. Some writers recorded teachings on the Kingdom of Heaven. All were closed with the pronouncement by Jesus that unless folks were to clear their plates and take on the heart of a child, then Heaven would be as far out of their reach as anything could be. It is then the one that we have come to call the rich young ruler placed himself in front of Christ.

His desire? He desired that eternal life Jesus spoke so much of. His question? He needed a checklist from Jesus, and Jesus gave it to him: No murder, no adultery, no stealing, no bearing of false witness, no defrauding, honor your parents and love your neighbor (all three accounts combined). As Jesus began to list these, one can almost see the Rich Young Ruler's chest swell as he began a mental checklist of everything that he had accomplished. Indeed, when Jesus finished listing from the Ten Commandments, the young man exclaimed, "All these things I have kept since my youth!"

Though Jesus was finished with the Big Ten, he wasn't finished. The young man was incomplete. He had held to the form and missed the function. He needed a throne change in his life: riches off/God on. He couldn't do it. Not then and there, at least. He realized his standing. Deflated he walked off. We don't see him again in Scripture. We'll have to wait to see the final outcome.

But Mark tells us something directly that Matthew and Luke do not:

And looking at him, Jesus felt a love for him, and said to him, "One thing you lack: go and sell all you possess, and give to the poor, and you shall have treasure in heaven; and come, follow Me."

Did you see it? It was the love that Jesus had for this young man. We have the example, now what do we do with it? We learn from it. We learn what love is at times and, just as important, what it isn't.

I don't know about you, but I really do enjoy the times we live in. I like the advances in medicine and all that it brings to the table. I like air conditioned vehicles here in West Texas in the summertime. I like multimedia and the ease at which we can procure food. I like computers and ATM machines. But, like you, I don't like everything. Some items are damaging.

I don't like the idea of toleration. It is killing the church.

Scriptures say some things are just wrong because God said so. The world tells us to lighten up and celebrate any and everything. I don't like excuses, either. They're like bellybuttons these days. Everyone has one and they're all being worn out front. It is the prelude to justification for every wrong doing and shortcoming that folks refuse to work on. Last, but certainly not completing a list by any means, I don't like soft, squishiness. I'm not referring to love movies with heart string tugging dialogue, but the tiptoeing around folks because we 'might hurt their feelings.'

Don't get me wrong. Brash, brazen and bold behavior is both uncalled for and, as we have considered in earlier chapters, un-Christlike. It simply has no place in the local church where you are. Handling truth in the way it was meant to be handled is not wrong. Out of love, notice what Jesus didn't do with the Rich Young Ruler. He didn't say, "Wait!" He didn't run after him and offer him a Plan B, for there was no Plan B. Jesus didn't ask him how he felt and then try to build up his self esteem. For Pete's sake, lopsided self esteem was this young man's problem to begin with!

However, don't miss the message of love here. Jesus' love for this fellow was strong enough that he told the man straight up just what was amiss in his life. He didn't yell at the Rich Young Ruler, belittle him or rip off his head and shout down his throat. He simply, out of love, explained the way of God more accurately to him. Can we do less?

How many folks have we let walk down a potentially fatal road because we did not share the truth with them (either not knowing the truth ourselves or afraid or didn't care)? How many folks have we watched die on the John chapter 15 vine because we thought that to correct them would not be showing love? I believe that we can all see where this line of questioning is going. Love is proactive, it is not simply a feeling.

Compare this to a love between a husband and a wife. By this I mean a husband and a wife. It is different than any other type of love on the face of the earth. We love our children, but spend our parental time preparing them to leave home for a successful life away from us (another story if you don't!). The love we have for our animals is, well, for animals. The love between a boyfriend and girlfriend is googly and full of hormones. I mean husband and wife.

Those of us who have been married long enough that we count time in decades know from where I speak. We travel along in life. We have fun together. We laugh and have good times. We have silly times. We have gut wrenching times that we simply have to hold on to each other so as to not go insane. There are short periods of time in which we feel that spontaneous combustion in the other would not be out of line, but we never stop loving.

This loving will also include times of corrections and suggestions and even putting our foot down.

Not in a mean way. We don't physically, emotionally or psychologically abuse each other. Not in a true, two way marriage. If we do, it is called spousal abuse and that is why we have coined the phrases, *going to jail and getting a divorce!* We do it in a way that will ultimately benefit our spouse. But by and large, we don't show love in the church family that way. Too many excuses. We're afraid that we might step on some toes and hurt some feelings. We're afraid that we might not have adequate information and wrongfully accuse someone of something that they just didn't do or say. We're afraid that we might drive someone off from the Lord (as if walking away from God is any different). In short, we might be wrong.

And we just might! But think about that marriage situation. Sure, at times toes are stepped on wrongfully and feelings are hurt over bad information. Sure, it might be quiet around the house for an hour or two (or day or two), but in the end the relationship is stronger and soon forgotten, replaced by fun times and happy days.

As far as love, we excel in areas. I've witnessed, as you have, folks and families experiencing death, disease, disaster, fire, flood and a host of other calamities that just don't seem to go away. We rush in with food, friendship, taking care of children, washing clothes and dishes, mowing lawns, passing the hat and continually rising above and beyond anything that we could wildly imagine on a good day. Nothing wrong with that. In fact, there is everything right with it. But we must excel in the other areas of love, also. Compare the next two verses and see if the connecting link of love doesn't stand out:

... let him know that he who turns a sinner from the error of his way will save his soul from death, and will cover a multitude of sins. Jas 5:20

Above all, keep fervent in your love for one another, because love covers a multitude of sins. I Pet 4:8

James, in his style of writing, calls turning a sinner back parallel to covering a multitude of sins. Peter says that love is the actual covering. If we apply the rules of syllogistic logic to these two verses we come up with one conclusion: Turning a sinner from the error of his way is equal to (or is an act of) love, pure and simple. The challenge remains and is twofold. Do we love our brothers and sisters in the church enough to turn them back from the error of their ways? When they turn us back, will we see it as an act of love?

We know love by this, that He laid down His life for us; and we ought to lay down our lives for the brethren. But whoever has the world's goods, and beholds his brother in need and closes his heart against him, how does the love of God abide in him? Little children, let us not love with word or with tongue, but in deed and truth. I Jno 3:16ff

We are members of one another and, therefore, are mandated to welcome and love one another. If mandated to live this way, we must pursue, not hinder these one another commands.

Questions for thought or discussion:

1. List five actions that you believe signify welcoming.

2. How many of the actions above took place in the church building? Why?

3. What attitudes should precede disciples loving each other?

4. Do you think disciples can love each other without any emotional bonds toward one another? Why or why not?

5. Describe different behaviors that you believe prevent disciples of Christ from loving each other as they should.

Endnotes:

[13] If context vs. pretext, rules of interpretation, and other tools are foreign to you, or you need to brush up on 'How To' of Bible study and interpretation, then read my book: ***Bible Survival Manual: Mystifying to Manageable*** from ***www.bookcrafters.net***. It is well worth it...

And If Your Brother Sins. ..

This subject may be the most misunderstood, malpracticed and most widely circumvented command that Christ gave his church. If mandated to live this way, we must pursue, not hinder this crucial Body Life command.

While attending Bible Boot Camp (*a.k.a.* Seminary), I accepted the responsibility of working with a small church. One of the first items on my list was to tour, or rather scrounge around, the church building where I would be maintaining an office. During my digging around the building as new preachers tend to do, I found a small black ledger in the pulpit. Believing it to be pertinent to my duties as the current pulpit guy, I began to meticulously read the entries that dated back for almost forty years. In it I found checks written for benevolence, funeral information, baptism records, gospel meetings and repairs on the building. I also found disturbing notes regarding some in the family.

The entries were documented and signed by a 'steering committee' and the votes by a show of hands in the church family were recorded. Names were listed with the vote tallies. Next to each of the tallies was the single word disfellowshipped. If this word doesn't hold any meaning for you, then I will share with you that other churches call this by its other name: excommunication. Instead of the one sheep being brought back to the ninety and nine (as described in Luke 15), it is the one sheep being driven out of the fold to face its fate.

During my teenage years, the church that I was attached to would each year in the springtime have what had come to be called, unofficially, Black Sunday. The attendance that Sunday morning was even worse than Superbowl Sunday. On the spring cleaning Black Sunday, the elders would get up in front of the church family and read the names of the long gone members that the elders had decided to disfellowship by a majority vote. They had been so long gone that the majority sitting in the pews had never heard of them. Any number of us could have (and maybe did) passed them on the street and never recognize them as being a former brother or sister.

One afternoon, while sitting in a much later branch office, I found myself on the phone with a woman--a very angry woman--trying to talk to her about her soul. She simply wouldn't listen to what I had to say. She held a letter in her hand dismissing her from the church I was preaching for and ministering to. Unless the same men who wrote that letter many years ago were to send her another letter apologizing, she simply wouldn't hear about it or discuss it in any way. For the next several years I never saw that woman cross the church house doorway. Of the three men who signed the letter, one was dead, one suffered from Altzheimer's and the other--though not a church leader any more --wouldn't discuss the matter.

In other places I have worked, I have mentioned church discipline in every conceivable setting from small groups to Sunday school classes to leaders' meetings. Almost without fail, the mere mention of the subject causes those in the room to visibly tense up. Eye contact goes away. Heads get cocked to the side. The fidget factor goes sky high. Everything imaginable begins to come out of folks' mouths:

"Well, we haven't had to do that around here in a long time. Just don't have the occasion to need to. Folks just sorta go about their daily rat killin', you know."

"Lots of folks got upset the last time that we did any disfellowshipping. Lost one or two families over it. You know, we have extended families here in the church. Boot one, and you run the risk of showing them all the door."

"We know that it is in the Bible, but it's not something that we are entirely comfortable with around here. It's hard enough to get the church to vote on what kind of carpet they want in the fellowship room much less voting folks out of the church! We would have to think hard on it."

"We should be about our Father's business of saving folks,

not kicking them out of the church. Bible says we ought to love one another, you know."

The popular view of church discipline today is akin to sacrificing a pig on the altar. Notice that I said the popular view of church discipline today. What comes to mind today, and what is generally practiced, is about as tasteful as a mouthful of raw minnows. However, the popular view of church discipline oftentimes has little in common with what Jesus intended for his church.

The totality of church discipline can be found in Matthew chapter 18. It would be well advised to read that chapter at this time in its entirety. While reading, note three distinct items concerning church discipline:

1. Church discipline falls into two parts
2. Church discipline is carried out in three encounters
3. Church discipline culminates in whole church business

In reviewing the above three items, allow me to jump ahead for the sake of setting up some roadblocks. Slow and steady would be the order of the day in this section. If we run too fast through the idea of church discipline, we will not all be on the same page when it is all over and we will simply do and believe what we have always done and believed. You know the rest of that: If you always do what you've always done then you always get what you always got. Poor English, to be sure, but it speaks. We've got frustrated church families sitting in frustrated church buildings on frustrated pews when it comes to the idea of discipline, so often we feel it is better to just let it all alone and do nothing.

But Jesus didn't speak about this subject just to hear his teeth rattle. No, he had a purpose. That purpose is twofold and can be seen in the two parts. The first part of church discipline is redemptive in nature. The second part is preventative. Both parts are distinctly seen in Matthew chapter 18.

The three encounters of church discipline can be seen clearly outlined in Matthew, also. We will take the time to break each one of them down. Note that in all of Matthew chapter 18, at no time did church discipline land solely into the hands of the elders, the preacher, pastor, committee...or a vote. Indeed, pastors and elders and deacons and committees and votes are never even mentioned in the entire chapter. Somewhere along the way, we have oftentimes placed them in there by themselves for various reasons. Because the idea of church discipline being an elder or leadership duty is fully entrenched in our thought patterns, this will be brought up again.

Again, let me state that the idea of church discipline is not tasteful overall. It ought to hurt us to think about having to go that far (part two) with a brother or a sister. It ought to cause us to feel pain at the deepest level, thinking about having to carry out discipline to its fullest extent (part two, encounter three). If you ever find someone who is gung-ho on the idea of rushing into church discipline simply to carry it out, then that person needs to be directed back to the parable in Matthew chapter 18 of the Brain Dead Servant that we have already examined.

Incidentally, Jesus had just finished giving his teaching on church discipline in Matthew 18:20. The first word in verse 21 is the Greek word *tote*, meaning *at that very same time*. It was Jesus' teaching on discipline that caused Peter to begin to think about forgiveness and ask the question, "Lord, how often shall my brother sin against me and I forgive him? Up to seven times?" It is that question that served as the launching platform for the Brain Dead Servant. Church discipline is serious. It is biblical, but serious. It is not for the gung-ho. There is caution and prayer and maturity involved, as we shall see. There is forgiveness involved, as we shall see. Forgiveness doesn't come easy to everyone at every time. The idea behind discipline demands it among one another. It is a part of Body Life.

As we delve into Jesus' teaching, let us not detach it from the context in which it was given (you did read Matthew 18, didn't you?). Jesus had been asked the question again as to who would be the greatest in this yet to be fully understood kingdom of God. Answer is simple: humble yourself like a little child...or forget it. Want to fuss and pick and try to be the greatest? Then keep on keeping on, for your reward will be here on earth in the chief seats and seen among men. However,

Heaven will only be a whisper when it is all over. Be humble, get the light off yourself, put down the horn, concern yourself with others, keep the body pure.

And by body here, Jesus means the church. Yes, we should pay close attention to ourselves personally, but Jesus has in mind the church family here. Eye bad? Dig it out and cast it off, for Heaven is in the balance for the remainder of the body. Foot not working properly? Cut it off and place it with the eye, for the bad foot is like a vortex for the rest of the body.

Jesus then focuses attention on the little child he had with him, with a warning. The warning, by this time, is clear: Don't mess with the body. The body is made up of people who have humbled themselves like little children. When a person, or people, mess with the body-- or attempt to mess up the body by their behavior and lifestyle, all the while claiming to be part of that body-- they mess with the very mission of our Lord and his church. That mission is to seek and to save that which was lost. It is so much the mission of the church that the church doesn't even deal with 'acceptable losses.' One sheep missing? Go get one sheep. Rejoice when found.

Then Jesus gives us the teaching that we need in order to remove the eye and the foot that is diminishing the overall performance of the body. Without this specific teaching, we would be left to our own devices and inventions. In some areas this is not so bad. The Bible directs preachers to preach the word. We've invented pulpits, half hour time slots, suits and ties, raised platforms for us to stand on, microphones for us to shout in, overhead projectors to draw on, background images, computer generated images,... and the list goes on. Nothing wrong with these inventions and aids--as long as the Word of God is preached and not compromised. Repeat--as long as the Word of God is preached and not compromised.

Jesus didn't see it that loosely with church discipline. Without specific commands and parts, we would be left to the thought for the day such as steering committees, elder-only disfellowshipping, votes by the majority, letters of dismissal, consensus of a committee, Black Sundays, and a host of other un-biblical nonsense. There was a time, not long ago as man counts time, that we would have drawn and quartered the heretic. The method is not for us to devise. God has spoken on it. He outlined it for us in Matthew chapter 18, verses 15-20. Six verses that we need to slow down on, examine, then vow to follow. Two parts with three encounters. Let's examine the first encounter.

And if your brother sins. We wonder at that statement. It is not so much *if* we sin as *when* we sin. It is probably an everyday occurrence with those of us who are honest enough to examine our lives against the standard of God's Word. Maybe it is just the sins that someone else sees?

For sure, as life goes here on earth, there are just a certain amount of things that I can do that neither you nor anyone else will see. Maybe someone will see, but they are as far away from God as east is from west and they don't even see it as a sin. Certainly, the things that go on between my ears are not on display (for a while, at least) so no one can see those sins. What is Jesus talking about here? If he means every sin committed, then our phone lines would be jammed with each of us calling the other to tell about something we saw them do. We would no more hang up our phone than it would ring--and someone would be on us.

This is the sin that breaks fellowship with God, the straw that broke the camel's back. Not all *sins* do, contrary to some folk's belief. *And thank God that not all do! Thank God that there is the continual forgiveness we enjoy while walking in the light! Thank God that He left us passages like First John chapter 1 that we can derive hope from.* But there can come a point when we turn off that path of light and onto a dark path. That is the willful sin with full knowledge of its consequences that Jesus is speaking of.

It is not the sister or brother that finds them self in a compromising position on a weekend date. It is the sister or brother that knows full well that circumventing God's plan of marriage by simply exercising a noncommittal, sex oriented lifestyle of 'shacking up'--but doing it anyway despite all the knowledge that it is outside God's will and wishes for his kids.

It is not the brother or sister who makes a bad business decision based on the greed of the moment. It is the brother or sister that enters into a business arrangement or decides to carry out business in a way or vocation that even the world regards as wrong. That's right, the world does see things as wrong at times.

It is not the parent that gets angry and frustrated with the child or spouse in an isolated incident, screaming loud enough for the neighbors to become worried. It is the one who repeatedly blisters the children and pounds his wife's face into ground round because he's the 'man of the house and doesn't care what you (the brethren) think.'

This list could go on, and does every day. These are examples that, hopefully, will get us on the same page. Too often we call it, "Well, that's just the way that they are..." John called it the sin unto death in his first letter.

If anyone sees his brother committing a sin not leading to death, he shall ask and God will for him give life to those who commit sin not leading to death. There is a sin leading to death; I do not say that he should make request for this. All unrighteousness is sin, and there is a sin not leading to death. I Jno 5:16f

...but if we walk in the light as He Himself is in the light, we have fellowship with one another, and the blood of Jesus His Son cleanses us from all sin. I Jno 1:7

Take the time to fully grasp what John is telling us in the first Scripture listed. I will forever be grateful to Gerald Paden for introducing me to Sam and Dave. Not the R & B Soul Group from the sixties, but just two folks called Sam and Dave. We insert them into the First John 5:16f passage and get things a little clearer:

If Sam sees his brother Dave committing a sin not leading to death, Sam shall ask and God will for Sam give life to Dave. There is a sin leading to death; I do not say that Sam should make request for this for Dave. All unrighteousness is sin, and there is a sin not leading to death. Slightly Revised!...and thanks, Gerald!

Substituting real names for the pronouns helps put this verse into perspective. Some translations didn't do a very good job at this point and the substitutions make no sense. This is why, dear Christian, that in order to do intensive, reaping,

Bible study, we need to get into the habit of reading out of several translations.

The second one was listed to remind us that we sin all the time, yet the majority live their life trying to walk in the light. The first was listed to remind us that there can come a time when sin reigns in a person's life, and that spiritual life is finally snuffed out. It is that snuffing out that Jesus was referring to in Matthew chapter 18.

How do we know? If we jump ahead in Matthew, we will note that if all goes well we will have won a brother. Won. You can't win something that you already have. You either have to have never had it--or have had it and lost it. It is the lost brother that Jesus speaks of. It is the sheep #100 of verse twelve. It is coin #10 and the willfully wandering boy of Luke chapter 15. It is the severed disciple, severed by his own choice and doing-- despite all his knowledge of God's will.

But let's jump back to the beginning, to the first encounter. You see a brother in such a circumstance. These circumstances are not hard to decipher. They are manifest by anger, sarcasm and avoidance of the family. It's the kind of circumstance that finds you talking to someone outside the church and you mention, "Yes, he goes to church where I do," to which the unsaved replies, "He does?!? You could have fooled me!"

And if your brother sins, go and reprove him in private; if he listens to you, you have won your brother. Matt 18:15

Two things to note about the first encounter. The first is, it is a private matter. Why? Because it just is, by God's design. Maybe you are wrong. You just might be. Certainly the fear that you may be wrong is forefront as you knock on his door or dial his telephone. By God's design, the first encounter is a one on one. The severed disciple is the first one, so who is the second one? Look again: "If your brother sins, go...if he listens to you... "Who? You! ...and the key word is brother."

It cannot be overstated here: If the first encounter is circumvented, then the whole process, up to and including the third encounter of part two (that we haven't even reached yet) will become more than simply botched, rather, it will become a disaster. There are too many disasters listed in the

Allelon: One Another

annals of church history. It is time that the disasters cease. God commands that you and I deal with our brothers and sisters. We hire preachers in our churches and appoint elders to lead, but God never allows us to shirk our responsibilities wholesale to one another. This area is no exception.

"But it isn't pleasant," one always says.

No, it isn't. But where God commands, we have no choice but to obey. He has a plan in mind that works. We need to work his plan. The time has come to let pastors and elders off the hook for the things that we have the responsibility for. When we circumvent and the disaster comes, that disaster will always include the finger pointing to the pastors and elders that we shrugged the task off onto in the first place. Moving outside the will of God always mushrooms--in a bad, bad way.

For reasons that will not be fully covered in this work, the Sunday morning attendance for worship is the last item to go from a person's life. Before the brother or sister succumbs fully to functional breakdown (*i.e.* just quits coming to church), prayer and Bible reading will have long been out of the picture. Put these two together and you will get conversation with God. Prayer--you talk, He listens. Bible reading--He talks, you listen. As with, for instance, a marriage, if the conversations cease it isn't long before the door opens and one is leaving with a suitcase, never to return. Physically being in the house is the last thing to go. So it is with a disciple. Being in the church house is the last thing to go.

So the brother quits coming. If the allelon passages are not being practiced fully in a church family, it will be a while before someone notices that the brother isn't there on Sundays. If the totality of a church's carrying out of the allelon passages is shaking hands on a Sunday morning, then it is often too late for what usually comes next.

A minister or perhaps a secretary begins to notice that the brother has missed consecutive Sundays. At this point, a letter or card is mailed out expressing the fact that the 'church' (in reality, the number crunchers) missed that person in worship. Another week goes by, or perhaps two. It is turned over to the visitation committee or the task is wholesaled to the minister or elders.

Church attendance long outlived the relationship with God by several weeks or months. Nonattendance is now approaching a month and a half to two. We all, at this point, know the story: the person has now reinvested their time and isn't moved easily. Sin is always involved in someone leaving the Body of Christ. It may not be murder or adultery. It may just be the sin of severing the tie with God through disenchantment, disappointment, immaturity, pressures from life, or a combination of any or all as we are well warned about in the parable of the soils with the "worries of the world and the deceitfulness of riches and the desire for other things." It is always easier to pull someone back into the fold when Body Life is alive and breathing in the local church.

So your brother sins. Jesus doesn't say that it has to be against you. He doesn't put the qualifier on it that you have to witness it. In fact, we rarely do, but we find out. Jesus also never gives us the out at this point of taking it to the attention of the preacher, the elders or other brothers and sisters. It is intended to be on the one to one level. And it should remain there.

Why? Well, the correct answer is that Jesus said so.

However, let's look at this thing from a human standpoint. You are the one caught in sin. You are the one who broke their ties with the Lord. You are the one who's doorbell suddenly rings on a Thursday evening while you are watching television... Now we get the picture. It is a merciful God who designed church discipline this way. No bulletins, no megaphones, no e-mails. Just one brother to another, trying to retie the lost back to God.

The objections usually apex with someone stating that because of their tongue tangling, bumbling, ineptness that they might drive someone away from the Lord. That person won't, for the one brother has already severed ties. How can one, who is speaking from the heart, drive someone further away? We may not know what to say exactly in that instant when we push the doorbell or begin dialing the seven numbers on the phone, but we can speak of the love of God and the dangers of an unbelieving heart. And here's a novel item: before we ring that doorbell or phone, we might just stop and ask God to help put the words in our mouth. Try it. It has worked for me, and it has worked for the brothers and sisters that taught the concept to me.

And remember, you might be wrong. You might have called something wrong or heard wrong or figured wrong or you're operating off of half truth. But if done correctly, it is still between you and the one you are standing there talking to. To say, "Brother, I'm really sorry. You can see where I was coming from. I hope that this doesn't make a dent in our relationship. Again, I'm sorry and let's go have a cup of coffee. I'll buy," (you better). End of story, just as Jesus wanted it to be.

Or you might be in a Romans 14:1-15:7 situation and what you call wrong isn't wrong to him and you have to call it a draw. Again, at that point it is over and done with. You may want to set up a time when the two of you can sit down and study this thing out--one of you just might have to change, and it might be you!

Or the person is wrong, dead wrong. Even the pagans would call it--whatever it is--wrong. Wrong to the point that he laid his salvation down and walked away from God. If he listens to you, you have won a brother. He is tied back to God, relationship restored. God's way once again worked, whether the brother listened to you or not. A note about end run plays. Some elders and preachers pick up on the plays and some do not. In the past, I've had many try to execute an end run. Some successfully and some not. Here's how it goes:

A preacher is busy in his office trying to work on Sunday's lesson when there is a knock at the door. Putting aside his Bible, Thayer's Greek/English Lexicon, Vine's, and two commentaries while hitting the save button on the computer, he opens the door where stands Sister Susie. Sister Susie has a pressing question that she needs direction on. She wanted to call, but really thought that face to face would be oh so much better. It is the six seemingly harmless words, "Can I ask you a question?" The preacher is always ready, in season and out, to give an answer to those who ask.

"It's probably something that I shouldn't ask, and I think I know what you are going to tell me but I was just wondering what to do with a certain situation or should I say one of the members here. I think it is really bad."

Interest roused. Ego awake. Preacher asks her to sit down. He does, and crosses his legs while grabbing his Bible off the corner of the desk. "It's about ol' Brother Whitley. I know what you're going to tell me I need to do but I feel like in this instance I might need some guidance from you, the preacher, since you deal with this stuff every day and study all the time." Uncrosses left leg and crosses right. Puts on glasses and tells her to go ahead, since she is looking for biblical guidance.

"I heard him say. . . I saw him do. . . People are telling me that he. . . It has come to my attention. . . Did you know?. . . I know for a fact that. . ."

You pick. It doesn't matter. The words come flying out of Sister Susie's mouth and, BAM!--end run play! Successful at that! Touchdown follows and the ball is now in the preacher's court. Encounter #1 successfully thwarted in the grand scheme of church discipline. What is soon (and sure) to follow will be the biggest mess that the preacher has gotten himself into since the last potluck! Doesn't have to be preachers, for there have been many successful end run plays around the elders in any given church.

"No," a preacher or elder will object, "I simply will counsel her and then not say anything to ol' Brother Whitley." Perhaps you won't, but a dollar to a donut says that the first words out of Sister Susie's mouth to ol' Brother Whitley will be, "Well, I was talking to the preacher the other day and he said..."

The mess is on!

Why do we do it? By we I mean preachers. I mean Christians. I mean Pastors. I mean Ministers. I mean elders. Because by and large we have not given ourselves over to doing this thing called Encounter Number One the way that Jesus intended it by design. We have all kinds of excuses from 'it hurts,' to 'it isn't pleasant,' to even 'what if I'm wrong?' I'm convinced (because God designed it) that if we were to commit ourselves to doing the first encounter the way that Jesus outlined it, attrition would be dealt a hearty blow. Let's examine the second encounter, which is still in part one of church discipline.

But if he does not listen to you. Because of our fears, most of us expect this to happen. And sometimes it does. It doesn't surprise God when it happens, that is why he devoted a whole encounter to the fact that someone just may not listen to you. Here is the verse in its entirety:

But if he does not listen to you, take one or two more with you, so that by the mouth of two or three witnesses every fact may be confirmed. Matt 18:16

To begin with, let's examine the witnesses. These particular witnesses are not witnesses to the sin. No, no, no! They are witnesses to this second encounter. If the witness was of the sin that broke fellowship with God, then many pagans would need to be about our Father's business. The biblical idea of witnesses goes all the way back to the Law of Moses and can be found in Deuteronomy 19:15:

A single witness shall not rise up against a man on account of any iniquity or any sin which he has committed; on the evidence of two or three witnesses a matter shall be confirmed.

In the first encounter, there is no qualification for the one. It is simply the person who first decided it was time to ring the doorbell. However, in regard to who is a witness today, one must heed such passages as listed here from the New Testament:

*I say this to your shame. Is it so, that there is not among you **one wise man** who will be able to decide between his brethren, but brother goes to law with brother, and that before unbelievers? I Cor 6:5f*

*Brethren, even if a man is caught in any trespass, **you who are spiritual**, restore such a one in a spirit of gentleness; each one looking to yourself lest you too be tempted. Gal 6:1*

Emphasis mine, but it should show us that this is no place for the spiritually immature, the weak, the unfruitful or, perish the thought, the gung-ho. Rather, this is the place of the mature, the fruitful, the wise and prayerful men and women of God, who have at the core of their heart the one lamb, miles from pasture, who keeps running farther away every time the herder approaches.

Notice that in the above verses, plus looking back at Matthew, there are a few words that are noticeably absent (here we go!): Elders, pastors, ministers, preachers, committees, bulletins or web sites, and one gets the picture. There certainly might be an elder or two or a preacher sprinkled in there somewhere among the one or two witnesses (but there certainly isn't a bulletin or committee sprinkled anywhere in there!). To insist that the witnesses be the elders is to insist (be dogmatic) on something that Jesus simply did not say. Arguing for something that isn't a Bible topic is never a good idea.

Also notice that there is increased publicity and social pressure in this contact. It is simply increased, not bulletin or Facebook material. It remains limited to the two or three of you and the one in question. All of the fears of botching it up, saying the wrong thing leaving the wrong impression and generally making a mess out of the whole situation will be greatly alleviated by the attendance of the witnesses. If they be spiritual indeed, then the directive that Paul gave Timothy on matters such as these will long have been a part of their lives:

Now flee from youthful lusts, and pursue righteousness, faith, love and peace, with those who call on the Lord from a pure heart. But refuse foolish and ignorant speculations, knowing that they produce quarrels. And the Lord's bond -servant must not be quarrelsome, but be kind to all, able to teach, patient when wronged, with gentleness correcting those who are in opposition, if perhaps God may grant them repentance leading to the knowledge of the truth, and they may come to their senses and escape from the snare of the devil, having been held captive by him to do his will. II Tim 2:22ff

They will be Jude's fire snatchers:

But you, beloved, building yourselves up on your most holy faith; praying in the Holy Spirit; keep yourselves in the love of God, waiting anxiously for the mercy of our Lord Jesus Christ to eternal life. And have mercy on some, who are doubting; save others, snatching them

out of the fire; and on some have mercy with fear, hating even the garment polluted by the flesh. Jude v20f

Time wise, there is no minimum or maximum time given between the first two encounters. The Bible is simply silent on the matter, but since we are to be scattered sheep seekers, it would do us well not to place a great amount of time in between the first two encounters. Why? Because of human nature. Out of sight is out of mind. Many times we want to give someone their space to 'think about it.' What that really translates to, oftentimes, is that if we put more water under the bridge, then it will become someone else's problem or somehow rectify itself--or go away. However, time in the form of 'a long time' is not in the best interest in this case. Case in point:

When I was young--actually, very young--about eleven, my friends and I decided that we needed different valve stem caps for our bicycle tires. One trip to the fire station and we saw what we had to have: Red ones! To be sure, we didn't even know that anyone even made red ones, but there they were. A plan was hatched. One of us would engage the firemen in questions about trucks, hoses and spotted dogs. The other would sneak around and remove red caps from the tires. We did, got extras, and proudly displayed them wherever we went. The extras were sold to other kids at a premium.

But I felt bad. Stomach ache bad enough to take mine off and take them back to the fire station [14]. I'm just sure that I told the firemen that I found them laying about the street, but I took them back just the same.

Forty plus or whatever years later I don't feel bad. I think it is childish yet funny. Sure, I'd get onto my kids if they were still that age and pulled a prank like that and I'd march them right down to the station... But you get my point. Time and water under the bridge, I've had my 'space' to think about it and I've told you what I think about it. Now consider something as horrible as sin which breaks all ties with God. We will feel bad about it for a while, then survival mechanisms will kick in, inclusive of rationalizations and reinvestment of time and energy, and we won't feel bad. When the witness brigade comes about, it will have little impact in our life.

In part one of church discipline, how much time should we allow between the first and second encounter? Soon. I repeat, soon.

If the brother or sister or couple or family listens to you, you have won your brother. You have snatched them from the fire. We've examined this verse before, but let's examine it again:

My brethren, if any among you strays from the truth, and one turns him back Let him know that he who turns a sinner from the error of his way will save his soul from death, and will cover a multitude of sins. Jas 5:19f

Part one, with its limited encounters and limited social pressure has been completed. I'm convinced that if the church of today were to strictly adhere to the first two encounters in the way that they were designed, then the so called 'church discipline' that we see too often today with its Black Sundays, committees, elder votes and letters of dismissal, will never rear their ugly, un-biblical heads. Think about it. Which of the two following scenarios would you rather have?

Scenario #1: You've done it. You've really done it. You knew it was wrong and you knew what the consequences between you and God would be. It is Sunday morning and you are still planning on going to worship, but deep down inside you know it is only a motion. Your brain and emotions seesaw between hurt, anger and sadness on the one hand and a whole string of rationalizations on the other. Now the worship hour is over. You took communion and sang all the old songs out of habit, now you need to see what Sister Mabel wants out of politeness-but at the same time, more than politeness. You've made up your mind that if she is going to ask you to help with the Annual Tasting Tea again this year, that you are going to have to decline. Your brain just can't take thinking about tasting teas or anything else right now. Anytime you start to think, your mind wanders back to that thing you did. Sister Mabel sticks her head out of a classroom and asks you to step inside. She begins:

"I'm sorry to take up your time. I promise I won't keep you very long. I've got something to say--or maybe ask--that

I might be wrong on. I hope that I am, and if I am I hope that you won't take me as a busy body or a tattle or something, oh, I don't even know where to start and I'm rambling. Anyway, I'll just say it...

Scenario #2: You've done it. You've really done it. You knew it was wrong and you knew what the consequences between you and God would be. It is Sunday morning and you are still planning on going to worship, but deep down inside you know it is only a motion. Your brain and emotions seesaw between hurt, anger and sadness on the one hand and a whole string of rationalizations on the other. Now the worship hour is over. You took communion and sang all the old songs out of habit, but you feel like a fish out of water now standing around in the foyer. It is time to leave. The following Sunday you do it all over again, and the next. Five or six Sundays pass and out of self preservation and sense of survival, you begin to believe that you could disappear from here and no one would notice. Next Sunday you sleep in, and the next. Your phone rings and it is the visitation committee wanting to know if you want a visit since 'everyone missed you last Sunday.' You tell them you have been busy and will get back into things soon. Nine and a half months pass and you get a letter, signed by the elders, stating that 'due to your absence from church, we have decided to remove you from the roles of the church that meets on the corner of Faith and Grace.' I don't know about you, but I'm willing to bet that more scattered sheep can be gathered in by the Sister Mabels than the Elders' Epistle. In the first scenario, the church family enjoyed Body Life. You weren't about to leave--as bad and as rotten as you felt before God--without seeing what Sister Mabel needed. In the second scenario, Body Life was limited to heidi-hos in the foyer on Sunday morning.

However, as strong as Body Life is in a church family, there still may come a time for the second part of church discipline, which has the third and final encounter in it.

And if he refuses to listen to them. Someone taught once that "If everything goes according to plan then it will never come to this final step." However, let's look at the overall picture once more before we examine this last encounter.

Someone sins. It is bad enough to break their ties with God, or so it is perceived. Joe or Jane Disciple has a one on one encounter as Jesus taught. They didn't run to the preacher or the deacons or the elders or put it in the bulletin or even talk about it in the weekly coffee cluster. However, the person who sinned didn't listen to them. Told them to buzz off, take a hike, none of their business what they did. Disciple gathered up three very mature disciples who have weathered many a lost sheep such as this. Four days later the second encounter took place as the tiny band pleaded for the soul of the severed. However, the severed did not feel like repenting at the time. It all went according to plan, Jesus' plan. Keep in mind that part two of church discipline is still part of the plan.

And if he refuses to listen to them, tell it to the church; and if he refuses to listen even to the church, let him be to you as a Gentile and a tax-gatherer. Matt 18:17

And why is this called part two? Simply put, it is now Whole Body Business. It is still redemptive in nature, asking for the restoration of the wanderer back to God and the family. However, it now takes on a preventative nature, also. Remember the bad eye and the lame foot? Just how is it that one unrepentant member, especially one who thinks he or she is still right with God, drag a church down? Remember, Jesus seemed to think that such a case could be.

A young sister in her mid-twenties, who had been in a saved relationship with God for nine years, decided it would be 'more economical' to move in with her boyfriend so the two of them could make ends meet. You know the drill. Her parents asked her to move back home and make ends meet there. She flatly stated she didn't care what they said or what God or the church taught. Meantime, she never missed a Sunday and continued to teach the First and Second Grade Sunday Morning Class.

Not a month passed by and she became pregnant. Still there was no marriage in sight, citing that they would wait to see if they were compatible for marriage. Parents of the young lady were shocked and embarrassed. Church was dumbfounded but every thing continued status quo. Meanwhile she left the father and moved in with another man. Soon it was time for a baby shower and the women of the church family busied themselves with announcements and preparing shower games and whatever else goes into those things.

Later, a friend of the young lady found herself in the same predicament. The young lady asked the church if they could throw a shower for her friend, just as they had done for her. Sisters got high behind and threw another shower for the expectant mother. Meanwhile, children not being as naive as we believe them to be, all the first and second graders became fifth and sixth graders--and before anyone knew it, they became juniors and seniors in high school.

When some of them began to 'shack up' with their respective partners, parents once again began to ask them to reconsider. They cited that it wasn't what God had intended. "It's not?" they all asked, "But it's OK with the church, now isn't it? By the way, would you be interested in throwing me a shower also? I forgot to tell you, I'm two months along."

And so the story goes. It was made up, but not entirely. It is, perhaps, played out again and again all across the nation. The ball got dropped between the first and second encounter (we'll call the parents the first encounter). No second encounter. No basis for a third. Folks got hushed and pretended. An entire generation of children began to make life choices based on what they experienced. The lampstand, placed in the church by Jesus himself, became ever so closer to being removed.

The apostle Paul had to intervene in the church in Corinth because church discipline was not being followed as Jesus had outlined it. In fact, First Corinthians chapter five is Paul usurping church discipline *on* a church for not practicing discipline *in* the church! Something horrible, even by today's standards in a sex saturated society, was being harbored in the church: someone was having a relationship with their father's wife. I don't know what the circumstances were. Was the father still alive? Was it a mother, or stepmother? Was the father and his wife divorced? We don't know. We do know two things about the matter. It was horrible even by Corinthian standards and the church was tolerating it.

Whoever it was, he believed himself to still be in full standing with God. He would sing *Paradise Valley* with as much gusto as the rest of the church on Sunday morning. He would take communion. He would lead closing prayers and help wait on the eucharist table. He could heidi-ho in the foyer with the best of them. Paul's command--remove him, for the long term outlook of the church didn't look bright following that road.

Even as Paul was instructing Titus how to lead a church family in Crete, he didn't deviate from Jesus' teaching on the matter of church discipline:

This is a trustworthy statement; and concerning these things I want you to speak confidently, so that those who have believed God may be careful to engage in good deeds. These things are good and profitable for men. But shun foolish controversies and genealogies and strife and disputes about the Law; for they are unprofitable and worthless. Reject a factious man after a first and second warning, knowing that such a man is perverted and is sinning, being self-condemned. Titus 3:8-11

Seems pretty swift when one reads it. One warning, two warnings, three warnings and you're out! No, to begin with, there is no time label on it. It doesn't necessitate an extremely slow time as we tend to do, but neither does it mandate that this take place within a half hour time frame. But do note, that the pattern is the same as in Matthew chapter 18, namely, two encounters. Paul calls them warnings.

So a brother or sister has had two warnings. They decide that they are more interested in the sin, and what it brings about in a season, than a relationship with God. They still insist that they are a 'member in good standing' with the church. The original person of encounter number one and the two witnesses agree that fellowship is broken in a willfully rebellious brother. What happens next?

The church is told. It is now Body Business. How this gets done, I don't know for the text doesn't say. It simply directs us to tell it to the church. Sunday morning? Best time to get all folks together. We will come back to expediency and caution in a moment, but for right now, let's explore why Jesus wants this to be whole church business.

For the same reason that the one went to the sinner in the first place: redemption. But there are other reasons, too. Remember the bad eye and bum foot? There is a lesson that Jesus wants the whole church to know, and that lesson is learned without leaving Matthew chapter 18: Keep the church pure. Do not mess with the bride of Christ. Better for a millstone to be hung about the neck...

At this point the lesson should be learned from the action. God wants each of us, and us as a group, to know that he will not tolerate willful sin in the life of a brother, especially if the whole church (knowingly or not) harbors that person as a 'member in good standing.' God doesn't want the Gentiles and Tax Gatherers looking at the local church, laughing and noting that it is no different in the church than outside of it. He's felt that way ever since the very starting point of the church with the case of Ananias and Sapphira recorded in Acts chapter five. Their judgment and sentence was swift, and was in the presence of all. There would be no mistake made by the rest of the church: lying to the Holy Spirit and testing the ability of the apostles would not be tolerated. Satan had indeed filled their hearts, but God, through his apostles, was not going to allow that to infect the fledgling church.

Negative impact on the new church? Many today would cite only the negative side of such an encounter and claim that if church discipline was carried out to the fullest that it would only tear down the church, both numerically and spiritually. If one were to keep reading in Acts chapter five on the matter, only church growth would be found. To be sure, a great fear fell upon those both in and out of the church, but a healthy fear that spoke of the seriousness of it all. Again, when one person, or a whole church, decides to carry out something God's way it will always end up right. In this case, it may or may not end up with someone being seen as a Gentile or a Tax Gatherer, but it will be right. I am convinced in my heart of hearts, with what little I've seen or heard about church discipline carried out in the biblical way, that if the church of God would simply resign herself to carry out this matter in the way that Jesus outlined it, that more folks would turn from sin in the first part of church discipline and it would never get to part two.

For now, let's return to expediency and caution in the matter of telling the whole church. Remember, if the whole church is told, then the whole church has a responsibility. I believe it can all be illustrated with a story.

Bill is a deacon in the local church. The church is not large by today's big city standards, but this particular church isn't in a large town. The boom-gone-bust town in the mountains now simply holds its own. Tourism is modest, but not like other places. Bill owns his own reshipping business. The church is active in the community. After much preparation, the church has begun small group ministry with a surprising outreach into the community. Over the last ten months, fourteen souls have been baptized into Christ through their efforts. Body Life has been gaining momentum and all folks try to hold a first century view on helping each other. This includes helping folks in this depressed economy town find work. Bill decided to step in and assist in this arena by giving jobs to two new disciples.

One of the newly hired disciples found something amiss in the reshipping business. Inventory was being set aside and disappearing. Pick-ups were being made after hours under suspicious circumstances. The new disciple asked Bill about it all. A friendly arm went around the new disciple's shoulder as Bill explained the finer points of lost inventory, stolen inventory, insurance claims and other things the newbie couldn't understand about reshipping. Several days later, the new disciple was 'explaining' this procedure to other folks down in the local diner, wanting to impress them on his knowledge of the business. The next day the new disciple was fired.

As the new disciple was telling this story in his small group meeting, one of the group's members, Carl, knew a mess when he smelled one. He wasted no time after the meeting to give Bill a visit. He let him know that what he was doing was wrong, it was illegal and it was sin--the worst kind that fires an honest, hard working brother in Christ--new or not--and smiles on the way to the bank. Bill didn't see it that way. He rationalized that insurance paid the bills, no one was out anything and even so, it was hard to make a living in that dried up miserable excuse for a town. Bill told Carl to mind his own business and stop minding Bill's store. Meeting over.

The next day, Carl called two other members at their homes. Erlinda was a long time accountant and a mature sister in the Lord. She had an awfully hard time even beginning to believe, let alone fathom, what had been done. She needed to chew on it for the better part of the morning. Fred was a deacon and one of Bill's good friends for many years. He saw everything clearly from the git-go, having been acquainted with the reshipping business. However, both were dumbfounded, but they agreed to accompany Carl on a visit to Bill. All four sat down as the meeting started with prayer. The pleading was cut short by Bill's anger as he literally held the door for the three intruders to leave--now.

Bill called them self righteous back stabbers. Bill slammed the door. Erlinda cried and Fred boiled in a mixture of anger and hurt. Carl silently drove. No one wanted to stop for coffee. They could barely even sort through what had taken place. They did, however, stop in front of Erlinda's house and prayed about the matter in earnest. All three agreed that Bill had overstepped the line and was willfully breaking ties with God.

The following Sunday morning, Bill was noticeably absent from services. His wife stated that Bill was 'feeling a little under the weather' but her face told it all. Fred had approached the elders that morning and told them he had a special announcement and would like for all visitors to be thanked for their attendance and then asked to dismiss themselves while the family carried out some family business. He explained what the announcement was about in order to, and only to, alleviate the fears of some type of bombshell being dropped on the church by a strange and disruptive announcement! We've all seen those from time to time.

The visitors were dismissed which consisted of three families on vacation and two seekers. Those who had invited the seekers departed with them, since they were the seekers' rides. Fred explained what was going on. There was shock. There was anger, for some sitting in the pews had been stolen from and their worst fears were being confirmed. There was some denial thinking perhaps the church had gone too far. There was immediate teaching from the elders (not the preacher) on the matter. It was decided that the whole church had the obligation to line up at the door of Bill's house and plead for his soul. Forty-three disciples, including Bill's wife, left the church building and headed for Bill's house.

The outcome? One of two paths. Either Bill was restored or he was not. The church did not drive Bill away, for Bill did that with his choices. The lesson was learned by the whole church: sin was not OK in the church, business or not. It did matter what the foot or the eye did in the family. Either way on the outcome, as we count outcomes, the method was a far cry from committees, Black Sundays, letters of dismissal for usually long gone disciples, elder-only disfellowships, and the unimpressive like.

Bill was not restored through the three encounter process. He slammed he door and threatened to call the police. How did the church respond? They saw him as a Gentile and a Tax Gatherer. How does the Bible say we should interact with a Gentile or Tax Gatherer? Seek and save that which is lost. Bill was not to be shunned. He wasn't to receive the cold shoulder in the grocery market or post office, but at the same time he wasn't to be viewed as a 'member in good standing' in the Lord's church. After two months passed, Bill was restored. More on that in a few paragraphs.

But what if the witnesses don't agree? What if one witness insists that it be dropped, one is unsure and the other is quite sure? What if two are very sure that fellowship was broken and sin was involved and the other wasn't sure at all? Jesus didn't leave his plan open ended:

Truly I say to you, whatever you shall bind on earth shall be bound in heaven; and whatever you loose on earth shall be loosed in heaven. Again I say to you, that if two of you agree on earth about anything that they may ask, it shall be done for them by My Father who is in heaven. For where two or three have gathered together in My name, there I am in their midst. Matt 18:18f

For sure, the last sentence has been grossly taken out of context at times. It is not a ticket for two ol' boys to hit the lake in their bass boat on a Sunday morning with a box of crackers and a bottle of grape juice. It is part of, and only part of, the church discipline process and concerns itself with the witnesses in the second encounter.

Let's return to the scenario: one witness does not agree on whether or not to take it to the church, for he or she does not agree that fellowship was broken. That sin is involved is not a question, but is a question on fellowship. They pray about it and still do not reach an agreement. Then they drop it, for they have their answer based upon the promise of Jesus in the Scripture above. Christ is the head of the church and is not divorced from the disciplinary action of the body. Christ is not asleep when it becomes prayer time. If there is no agreement, then drop it.

One witness is insufficient and an abomination according to the Law of Moses. What is an abomination to the Lord does not change with the covenants. God did not drastically change his nature somewhere between Malachi and Matthew. This promise of Jesus is what is termed practical inspiration (as opposed to plenary, which is the type of inspiration meant when we talk about writing the Bible) and should not be scoffed at. This is the *reddy rekkalexions* type of inspiration. They may reach the conclusion to take it to the church. Either way, Jesus promises that they will have their answer. The witnesses should be mature enough to abide by that answer when it is received.

Take note that this loosing and binding is not the same as in Matthew chapter 16. There the loosing is the Old Covenant and the binding is the New Covenant. In Matthew chapter 18, the loosing and binding is the revelation to the witnesses of the standing of the individual before God. One cannot mix these two verses based upon the similarity of the wording outside context (*cf* Jas 2:20 & Eph 2:8-10). Notice also that the pressure is taken off the disciplining procedure. The church doesn't decide, for God has already made the decision. As the whole body is involved in the third and final encounter, if the man repents, the whole body should be at the door to re-fellowship.

Let's now go back to Bill, who after two months was restored. Due to the pressure from the church and his wife, he decided to quit his shady business practices (illegal, really) and make money the old fashioned way: hard work. He determined to attempt to make right where he could. He called those in his church family he had personally hurt business-wise and laid out his restitution plan. One brother said not to bother, he was OK. Two others said they would be looking for the check in the mail. A fourth was furious and wouldn't speak to Bill and slammed the phone down.

On a Tuesday, Bill spoke directly to Fred and Carl about his need to 'go forward' on the next Sunday and ask forgiveness from the church. Both thought that it would be a grand idea, but as soon as they parted with Bill, they got the church family hot line working. By that same Tuesday evening, 27 different disciples had already been to Bill's house welcoming him back into the family of God. On Sunday morning, as the church sang the invitational hymn, *Just As I Am*, Bill stepped out into the aisle...

Even if what was written on Church Discipline had turned out to be over two hundred pages by itself, it would not have begun to scratch the entire surface of the matter. Church Discipline is a serious matter and a serious part of Body Life. Nothing can disrupt Body Life like a disruptive disciple who still sees himself in perfectly good standing with both God and the brethren. The answer, as Jesus taught, is simple: three encounters with increased pressure on each one. Unrepentance will bring about a casting or throwing down of the eye or foot. The Greek word *ballo*, or throw, carries with it the idea of peril involved. Infection of the body from within is difficult to overcome. It becomes systemic, and quickly.

But even if the church were to vow to carry out discipline in the manner that Jesus outlined, only to bungle it up by botched first encounters, poorly picked witnesses for the second and poor timing in 'telling it to the church,' it would still be much, much better than the way in which it is often carried out today. If mandated to live this way, we must pursue, not hinder this crucial Body Life command.

Questions for thought or discussion:

1. What is your understanding of church discipline? How (or is) is this carried out among the family where you worship?

Endnotes:

[14] Not bragging here. Only bragging about my parents and all godly parents anywhere. Deuteronomy chapter 6 (the *Sh'ma Yisrael*) is still poweful today. You teach kids the right, godly way to be and they will. Hard and fast rule? Of course not, except for the opposite--if we don't teach our children, or teach them garbage as a kid, then note how that one turns out.

Final Thoughts on Body Life

Jesus is the head of the church. As noted earlier, he could have planned something else for mankind but he didn't. The church was so important to him in his overall plan to save mankind that he was willing to come to earth and die for it--a most horrible death. Not in a sense of the physical type of death, horrible as that was. For you see, many men have been hung on crosses, locked in dungeons and crow cages to slowly starve, drawn and quartered and a host of unthinkable deaths. But Jesus' death was the most horrible of all and from a spiritual standpoint. He loved us enough that he was willing to take on the sins of all mankind only to have the Father turn his back on him for a moment in time. When Jesus cried, "My God, my God, why have you forsaken me?" he knew the answer. The answer was sin. Yours. Mine.

And sin is what Jesus wants out of the church and kept out of the church. That is where each and every one of us comes into importance. Without our daily and continual watching over each other through the various one another commands, sin will creep in, grab control one at a time, and soon sweep the church clean of all disciples. Sure the form may continue long after the lampstand has been removed but the outcome is the same. The songs and prayers may go out, but not up.

Cain asked God if he was his brother's keeper. Perhaps he genuinely didn't know the answer at the time. For sure, the human race was pretty new at the game, but we are not and don't even need to ask the question. If First Corinthians 12:18 is true (and it is), then God placed the folks around you on any given Sunday morning (Friday evening and Thursday afternoon) for a reason and that reason is mandated in Body Life--the vertical defined by the horizontal. Nowhere is this two directional relationship spelled out better in one verse than found in the last verse of James chapter 1:

This is pure and undefiled religion in the sight of our God and Father, to visit orphans and widows in their distress, and to keep oneself unstained by the world.

Yes, we have the mandate to keep ourselves unstained as we stand before God. Just as important, we have the mandate to be an integral part of other's lives. The word *and* that James uses is just as important here as it is in Isaiah 1:19, Matthew 5:12 and Mark 16:16 --one without the other is simply incomplete for the matter at hand.

We can sing, pray, give, listen intently to the sermons and take communion every Sunday. We can be there every time the church house doors fling open. Ministers can spend hours searching out a passage and bringing the best lesson with as much depth as they can (and we better!). As Paul said in First Corinthians chapter 13, we could give all our possessions to feed the poor, and deliver our body to be burned, but if we do not have love for the brethren, it profits us nothing. Earlier in the chapter he said that if we do not have love, the sound we make is akin to someone banging two trash can lids together in some spiritual back alley somewhere. A joyful noise, it is not. How we view our brothers and sisters, and ultimately how we treat them, is in reality how we will view God, regardless of what we say or how loud we sing *Just As I Am*.

The growth and health of the local church depends on the local church. There is not a program or a speaker or a secular book or a workshop or a worship style that will grow the church. The church grows the church as God works in her and through her. Whether the membership is forty, one-forty, four hundred forty or a thousand and forty, the church grows the church. We are members one of another.

Perhaps, in this day and age of not any real persecution to speak of, the church has grown apathetic. We try to speak of persecution in our Sunday school classes, comparing what we know from early church history to losing friends and lifestyles today--friends and lifestyles we need to do without anyway in our Christian walk! I'm not, in any way, advocating that we open up the colosseums again, complete with gladiators and lions, but am wondering if the lack of visible pressure against Christianity has allowed the invisible pressure of complaisance to settle in. We do church much like we do little league or a civic club. For many, it has not significantly changed their lives at all.

While in ministry school, we were challenged to read Sheldon's *In His Steps* not once, but once each year throughout the remainder of our time on earth. I kept up for at least five or six years. This work has been nothing more than that book but with a little more of a didactic swing. The book, fiction yet not, was a story of living out the question *What Would Jesus Do?* This book is more of *What Did Jesus Say?*--and where did he say it at? Sheldon's book is well over a hundred years old, yet timeless. This work was almost 20 years in the making. Time will see whether or not it is timeless, however, the Scriptures captured within this work are as timeless as anything can ever be.

When Christ returns, we will not be judged by (keyword = by) our attendance on Sunday. We will not be judged by our acts of worship when we all meet together, nor even be judged by our actions or our words (though these things will themselves be judged!). We will be judged by the words of Christ. John chapter 12 couldn't be any plainer.

So, we must K-N-O-W the words of Christ. We saw the importance of the word of God with Jonah. We see it in the 119th Psalm and in Deuteronomy chapters 6 and 28. Finally, as our western Bible closes, we see it in Revelation as one by one seven seals are broken from a throne room book in judgment against those who did--and continue to--oppose God's people and purpose.

This is neither an invitation to begin reading things into the Scriptures (isogesis) nor is it a directive that mandates we should find "something new" every time we open our Bibles (some thrive on this nonsense). It is, however, an invitation to go one level deeper in our understanding of God and his desire for us. The Bible is the only place that desire can be obtained with any degree of certainty.

Provided you learned anything new from this reading,

or reinforced something that had been sleeping in the back of your mind all along, there remains a question: What will you now do with this information?

About the Author

R F Pennington has interspersed careers, degrees and certification in oil and gas well drilling, law enforcement, clinical medicine and counseling. R F has held full time ministry positions for twelve years. He graduated from Sunset International Bible Institute and earned a Bachelors of Ministry from Theological University of America. For many years R F has focused on house church ministries and writing. R F and Dee make their empty nest in El Paso, Texas.

Published writings include this book, *Jude's Letter for Today's Path, A Healthy Thing Should Look Like This* and *The Bible Survival Manual: Mystifying to Manageable.*

All books may be obtained from online bookstores and www.bookcrafters.net.

CPSIA information can be obtained at www.ICGtesting.com
Printed in the USA
LVOW04s2116030914

402307LV00010B/96/P